Routledge Revivals

The Commerce of Nations

First published in 1929, this book was written to express the belief that nations' commercial policy and doctrines could best be explained by reference to their history. The author argues that this applies equally to legislation and theory, for example both the McKinley Act of 1890 and contemporaneous protectionism are examined as the culmination of a century's worth of legislative and theoretical progress. This edition is also updated from the original 1891 publication to take account of the effect of the First World War on the European and American tariff systems, and also how the preferential system of trade within the British Empire recast relations between Britain and its dominions.

T0293716

The Commerce of Nations

C.F. Bastable

Routledge
Taylor & Francis Group

First published in 1923
by Methuen

This edition first published in 2017 by Routledge
2 Park Square, Milton Park, Abingdon, Oxon, OX14 4RN
and by Routledge
711 Third Avenue, New York, NY 10017

Routledge is an imprint of the Taylor & Francis Group, an informa business

© 1923 C.F. Bastable

Publisher's Note
The publisher has gone to great lengths to ensure the quality of this
reprint but points out that some imperfections in the original copies may
be apparent.

Disclaimer
The publisher has made every effort to trace copyright holders and
welcomes correspondence from those they have been unable to contact.

A Library of Congress record exists under LC control number: 23011802

ISBN 13: 978-1-138-23120-7 (hbk)
ISBN 13: 978-1-315-31564-5 (ebk)
ISBN 13: 978-1-138-23125-2 (pbk)

THE COMMERCE
OF NATIONS

BY

C. F. BASTABLE, LL.D.

PROFESSOR OF POLITICAL ECONOMY IN THE UNIVERSITY
OF DUBLIN; EXAMINER IN POLITICAL ECONOMY IN
THE UNIVERSITY OF LONDON, ETC., ETC.

NINTH EDITION
REVISED BY

T. E. GREGORY, D.Sc. (Econ.) Lond.

SIR ERNEST CASSEL READER IN COMMERCE
IN THE UNIVERSITY OF LONDON

.

METHUEN & CO. LTD.
36 ESSEX STREET W.C.
LONDON

First Published		.	.		.	.	*November*	*1891*
Second Edition	.	.	.	.	.	.	*March*	*1899*
Third Edition	.	.	.	.	.	.	*May*	*1904*
Fourth Edition	.	.	.	.	.	.	*September*	*1907*
Fifth Edition	.	.	.	.	.	.	*April*	*1911*
Sixth Edition	.	.	.	.	.	.	*December*	*1912*
Seventh Edition	.	.	.	.	.	.	*October*	*1914*
Eighth Edition	.	.	.	.	.	.	*August*	*1917*
Ninth Edition, Revised	.	.	.	.	.		*1923*	

PRINTED IN GREAT BRITAIN

PREFACE TO NINTH (AND REVISED) EDITION

SINCE the publication of the eighth edition of this work the Great European War has thrown the whole tariff system of Europe into the melting-pot. At the same time the development of a preferential system inside the British Empire has completely recast the economic relations between this country and the self-governing dominions. I have tried to incorporate all the latest information with regard to European and American conditions into this work, but the situation changes so much from day to day that it is difficult to keep up to date. I have necessarily had to rely largely on the standard works on the subject of tariffs, and I have made full use of the invaluable information gathered together in the pages of the *Board of Trade Journal*. Students who desire a fuller acquaintance with theoretical questions may be referred to Professor Bastable's *Theory of International Trade* (Macmillan) and to my *Tariffs: A Study in Method* (Griffin).

T. E. G.

27th October, 1922

PREFACE TO FIRST EDITION

THIS book has been written in the belief that existing commercial policy and the doctrines respecting it are best explained by reference to their history. A method that has been so fruitful in all other directions of social inquiry can hardly be ineffective in this one.

Thus, to give instances, the McKinley Act (p. 77) is not properly understood until it is regarded as a single step in the legislation of a century. The Sugar Bounties (pp. 175-176) take us back to the continental system and the old colonial policy ; and a customs-union of the British Empire presents difficulties only known to those who have studied the effect of the differential duties. So it is also with plans for reciprocity. Their strongest refutation lies in the fact that they have been tried and failed (pp. 190-4). In like manner the most effective justification of the English free-trade system is supplied by the history of its introduction (Chapter VI).

What is true of legislation applies equally to theory. Modern protectionism should be studied in its development in order to see its connexion with ideas and sentiments unsuited for industrial civilization. Only in this way is it possible to understand how so many able and enlightened men have adopted a system that is notwithstanding injurious both to social and economical progress.

One result of this mode of treatment has been to diminish

the amount of space devoted to certain topics that are prominent in most works on the subject. Little is said about the Corn Law struggle, nor is the free-trade movement regarded as if it began and ended with Cobden. A few years can after all be but one stage—a highly important one it is true—in a movement that must in its entirety occupy centuries.

The absence of footnotes has prevented reference being made to the various works used ; but a general acknowledgment must here be given to those who have supplied so much of the material necessary for a study of the kind.

C. F. BASTABLE

Trinity College, Dublin,
November, 1891

CONTENTS

THE COMMERCE OF NATIONS

CHAPTER I

INTRODUCTORY

ONE of the most striking features of modern times is the growth of international relations of ever-increasing complexity and influence. Facilities for communication have brought about closer and more constant intercourse between the different countries of the world, leading to many unexpected results. This more intimate connexion is reflected in all the different sides of social activity. International law, that two hundred years ago was almost wholly confined to the discussion of war and its effects, now contains a goodly series of chapters treating in detail of the conduct of nations during peace. It draws the bulk of its materials from the large and rapidly growing body of treaties that regulate such matters, and form so many fresh links between the states that sign them. Literature, Science, and Art have all been similarly affected ; their followers are engaged in keenly watching the progress of their favourite pursuits in other countries, and are becoming daily more and more sensitive to any new tendency or movement in the remotest nation.

But, as might be expected, it is in the sphere of material relations that the increase in international solidarity has been most decisively marked, and can be best followed and appreciated. The barriers that in former ages impeded the free passage of men and of goods from country to country have been—it cannot unfortunately be said removed, but very much diminished ; and more particularly during the last fifty years the extraordinary development and improvement of transport agencies both by land and sea have gone far towards obliterating the retarding effects of legislative restraints or national prejudices. So little attention is ordinarily paid to the great permanent forces that govern the changes of societies, in comparison with the interest excited by the uncertain action of minor disturbing causes, that it is eminently desirable to emphasize as strongly as possible this continuous increase of international dealings. In spite of temporary checks and drawbacks, the broad fact stands out beyond dispute that the transfer of human beings from country to country which is known as "migration," as also the similar movement of goods described as "commerce," is not merely expanding, but, if periods sufficiently lengthy for fair comparison are taken, expanding at an accelerated rate.

We are happily enabled to form a conception of the extent of this latter movement with a degree of accuracy that is quite impossible in respect to other sides of social life. The growth of peaceful relations between states, the connexion and reciprocal influences of scientific and literary workers belonging to various nationalities, cannot, it is evident, be included within and comprised by any definite expression that would give a measure of their growth from time to time. The case of commerce is in this respect different. The elaborate and laboriously worked out statistics of official departments supply abundant *data* for a full and careful estimate not simply of the fact of extended trade, but also of its amount. To give a few illustrations which bear out this assertion, we may first take the case of England. A glance at the Board of Trade returns for 1913 shows, to take the last pre-war year as illustration, that the sum in values of imports and exports (re-exports included) for that year was a little under £1,300,000,000. These figures may at first surprise by their great amount, but they can easily be understood and compared with similar returns for previous years, and with the estimates of the amount of domestic trade, so as to give an approximately correct idea of the quantity and proportion of national wealth that is concerned and employed in this branch of trade. The foreign commerce of other countries was not on so extensive a scale. Owing partly to the natural advantages of situation, and to facilities for obtaining abundant supplies of raw materials, but also partly to the absence of legislative restrictions, the development of British commerce is by far the greatest that has yet been known. Germany had for the year 1913 foreign commerce to the amount of almost £1,000,000,000, while the American Union, whose policy is avowedly restrictive, and which possesses within its own territory most of the staple articles of industry, and is so far relieved from any pressing need for foreign commerce, showed for the year 1913, a sum of imports and exports of over £816,000,000. The financial dislocation caused by the war itself, and the alterations of territory induced by the Treaties of Peace, as well as the changes in the value of money, make post-war comparisons difficult. There has certainly been some decline in the real volume of world-trade, concealed though that has been by a fall in the purchasing power of money.

The figures just stated are not less impressive and much more readily comprehended than the most complicated tables giving the quantities and values of each of the innumerable articles that enter into the course of foreign trade and swell as total. They prove conclusively that this part of economic activity is one of the most potent of the factors which taken together make up the general industrial movement, and one moreover that cannot be put aside or neglected by anyone who desires to form an intelligent idea of the world's advance. It would be no doubt an error to follow the old mercantile belief and regard the amount of foreign trade as the sole and sufficient measure of national progress. Even for England domestic trade is on the whole much more important; it is far larger in extent, and it enters more closely into every part of national life—a statement that is still more unreservedly true of countries like the United States. The decline of foreign commerce may conceivably be accompanied by a more than counter-balancing expansion of internal trade; but this case so rarely occurs that it hardly requires notice as a practical limitation of the proposition that the enlargement of international exchanges is an indication, and in itself a part of economic improvement, and that in the long run there is a connexion between the smaller movement and the larger one of which it forms a part.

To explain the working of this part of the economic system, and to form a judgment as to the policy applicable to it, is the object before us. For the end in view, it is necessary to consider the principles or rather conditions on which international in common with all commerce is based, and more particularly the modifications that its special characteristics make requisite in the use of the laws of exchange for the purpose of interpretation. By adopting this course, a great many of the erroneous conceptions that interfere with the acquisition of a proper knowledge of the matter will be indirectly removed, and the groundwork of many fallacious arguments will be destroyed without the need of much formal refutation. The commercial policy actually pursued by nations will then claim attention, both in its historical development and its present position in the leading countries of the world. This review of former and existing state policy in respect to foreign trade will lead directly to a comparison of the methods pursued, and an estimate of their comparative efficacy in promoting national welfare; and in this connexion the various erroneous or incomplete theories that have influenced state action will be examined and criticized.

Before commencing the inquiry thus outlined, a preliminary difficulty may be removed. Without attempting to enter on the subtleties of the subject, for which there is no place, it is desirable to state expressly what is meant by *international* commerce. Our answer to that question is as follows: All commerce comes under the head of international which is carried on between persons resident in different political entities or units, even though—as in the case of England and India—they may stand in the relation of ruler and subject. This use of the term is at once simple and convenient; it accords closely enough with popular phraseology as well as with the more technical application made by official statisticians, who always separate such trade from domestic transactions, for which reason its special investigation is peculiarly suitable. Another reason in its favour is found in the fact that it is to this division of commerce that state interference on economic grounds has been almost exclusively directed. It follows that for the practical object of considering the effects of different lines of policy, there is a great advantage in confining our attention to a well-recognized area within which the agencies under examination have been chiefly employed.

The commerce of nations when regarded in the way just suggested is evidently liable to shrink or expand in proportion to the junction or division of political units. That is, in other words, its amount will in great measure depend on the number and distribution of the nations in the world. Thus, to give instances, the creation of Italian unity changed so much foreign into domestic trade; and if the formation of the German Empire had not a like effect, it was due to the fact that commercial unity had there been attained at an earlier date through the *Zollverein*, or customs-union. The separation of Holland and Belgium is an opposite instance, since by it there was an increase of foreign at the expense of domestic commerce. Statistical and other comparisons have been made more than usually difficult by the territorial alterations of Europe due to the war. Austria-Hungary has disappeared and new states have appeared in its place. Russia and Germany have suffered important losses of territory; France and Italy, Poland and the Baltic States have gained at the expense of the Central Powers, even if we leave the case of Czecho-Slovakia on one side. These particular cases, however, have hardly any effect on the general movement, if we take long periods into account. Whatever transfers may take place between the fields of home and foreign trade, the general facts and operating tendencies remain substantially unaltered; and for purposes of comparison a sufficiently correct allowance can be made with regard to the changes that occur within the periods to be compared.

CHAPTER II

LEADING FEATURES OF INTERNATIONAL COMMERCE

AT first sight it would appear that domestic or internal trade was by far the earliest, and that foreign commerce came in as a later addition, the result of more advanced economic development ; and if the statement is limited to commerce as it exists at present, and to the actual division of home and foreign trade, it is certainly correct. But in another and wider sense of the term it is possible to maintain the seeming paradox that the first exchanges were international (or rather intertribal). Recent investigations of the early history of law and institutions, such as those of Sir H. Maine and De Coulanges, tend to establish that the unit of primitive communities was the family, rather than the individual who occupies that position in modern times. The elaborate formalities of ancient law were suited to such a conception, and resemble the modes of commercial intercourse that are now retained only between states. The primitive kinds of contract are particularly interesting in this respect, since one of the most important of contracts—sale—is closely bound up with conveyance, the legal form of the fact of exchange whose economical bearings we have been considering. Without accepting all the details of any theory of the ancient contract of sale, or barter, it may be confidently held that it was hedged round with complex formalities, most of them indicating that the process was one that affected the community and required its sanction as a condition of validity. This can only be explained by reference to the comparatively small number of exchanges, which were not necessarily *within* any group, " as there property was held in common," and only took place between " house communities " or " tribes." Thus, if the conception of international trade may be so widened as to

6

include all dealings between groups or bodies, or between members of different groups, we may say with truth that it is the oldest and most primitive kind of trade.

The interest of this result is not purely historical; if it were so we might here safely neglect it. It has, however, a practical value, as it shows the long-continued working of conditions that are still potent in determining the course of foreign trade, and it to some extent throws light on the real source of much legislative regulation whose origin is now completely forgotten, but which has been produced by the old sentiment of tribal jealousy. The theory of international trade is concerned with the statics, rather than the dynamics, of the situation. What it attempts to do is to provide, firstly, a *general* explanation of the advantages of international trade, though in this connexion it is but re-echoing the general teachings of economic science on the subject of the advantages of exchange; secondly, its more specialized function is to explain the *particular* nature of the trade which is being carried on at a *given moment of time*: it tries, i.e. to explain why and when it becomes advantageous to exchange *given* products between *given* units or " countries."

Until very recently it was thought that this explanation involved factors which differed radically from those which were at work in internal trade. The theory of international trade, in the classical political economy, was a separate department of study, because it was thought that international and domestic trade were governed by different factors. The main differentiating element, it was thought, was the freedom of movement which existed inside a country, as compared to the relative sluggishness of movement of capital and labour between different countries. But two facts have contributed to make this distinction a false one, when applied to the actual situation. Firstly, the extent to which there was free movement inside a given country was usually exaggerated by the classical economists. Apart from natural differences of talent, of acquired skill, and the like, there exist in all countries barriers of a more artificial kind both for capital and labour; it is only necessary to mention trade-union restrictions and the barrier imposed on the movement of natural ability by lack of means. Secondly, the extent to which freedom of movement between countries existed was generally *under-rated* by the classical economists, and this under-estimation was continued by those who accepted their theories at a time when the facts on which the theory was originally based no longer existed. We are in fact bound to recognize that, from the wider point of view, international and domestic are both simply cases of exchange generally, subject to the same general laws, and that there is consequently no need to evolve a basically different theory to account for international trade, though the incidents of international trade may well demand detailed and special attention. In particular, we may take over from the classical theory on the subject the statement that the trade between two countries at a given moment is governed by " comparative cost," and our task here is to make clear the implications of this statement.

Let us deal first with a simple case. Suppose that the expenditure of £1 will enable either 10 units of article x or 8 units of article y to be produced in a given country A. Now suppose that in another country B an expenditure of £1 will enable either the production of 8 units of x or 10 units of y. The problem of international trade is simply this : Which commodity should be produced in which country ? And, having settled this : What is the net gain resulting from an interchange of the products ?

First, if *both* countries produce *both* objects, an expenditure of £4 will mean a total production of $18x$ units plus $18y$ units. If, on the other hand, A produces only x, and B produces only y, then an expenditure of £4 will produce $20x$ units plus $20y$ units. There is consequently a gain of $2x$ units plus $2y$ units. If the two countries *each* produced the *two* articles, they would between them produce that amount less. Consequently, they will each of them gain by concentration of production, providing that the articles can be exchanged between them on terms which will leave each of them better off than they would have been had the exchange not taken place. In country A, a unit of y is worth $\frac{10}{8}x$ units ; in country B a unit of x

is worth $\frac{8}{10}y$ units. Consequently, if the exchange takes place on the basis of A getting rather more than $8y$ units for $10x$ units from B, whilst B gets rather more than $8x$ units for $10y$ units from A, then not only will there be a gain to the two of them taken together, but a gain to each of them taken *separately*. The *terms* of the exchange in each given case depend on the relative bargaining power of the units concerned, but the limits of the exchange are given by the relative capacity to produce the articles exchanged. If both countries produce both articles at the same cost, obviously there will be no advantage in exchanging them ; if one country refuses to part with its product to the other except on terms which will leave the other no better off than it would have been if it had produced the article itself, again no exchange will take place.

The term "comparative cost" must not lead the student astray. The costs which are being compared are not the costs of the articles which *are* exchanged, but the costs in each country of the article which *is* being produced, and in part being exported, and the cost of the article which is not being produced, and in part therefore being *imported*. It is, of course, true that the articles which are imported and exported respectively are *components* of the comparisons which have been previously made, but the term "comparative cost" relates to the previous comparison. What we know is that the articles which are imported in each case represent those articles which, had they been produced at home, would have been produced at the lesser advantage, or, in other words, would have represented the smaller return for a given amount of effort. Thus if, in our illustration, x stands for cotton piece goods and y stands for silk goods, and A and B stand for England and France respectively, then we may say that whereas this country manufactures cotton more advantageously compared with silk, France manufactures silk advantageously compared with cotton. Since this country is better at cotton goods, and France is better at the production of silk goods, an exchange of products must result in benefit, if the difference in the productive capacity is at all significant.

In those cases where two countries exchange products which the importing country can only produce under circumstances of great difficulty, the advantages of such exchanges are obviously so great that no dispute can arise on the benefits afforded by international trade. But the advantages of such trade appear at first sight to diminish in those cases where one country possesses a superiority of productive capacity over the whole range of products which another country can produce. Will trade be carried on and, if so, on what basis ? It is very often feared that if one country can produce more cheaply than another in every direction, then that trade will be completely one-sided, and the inferior country will have to give up all trade. But this is an impossibility ; for sale cannot take place without reciprocity ; that is, it is impossible for one country to go on selling without taking something in exchange. But will it pay, not only the inferior, but also the superior country, to exchange ? An illustration will show that it will. A doctor may be a better gardener than the gardener whom he employs, but he may be a still better doctor, and he would lose if he did not restrict himself to the highest type of work which he could do. His advantage over the gardener is greatest not when he is acting as gardener, but when he exercises his functions as doctor. So a country may be able to produce everything better than another country, but it will pay it best to concentrate on those articles at which its comparative advantage is greatest ; whilst the inferior country must restrict itself to those products at which its comparative disadvantage is least.

The use of the doctrine of comparative cost in throwing light on the course and extent of international commerce is great. For it is on the existence of differences between costs when compared in the trading countries that the possibility of any trade taking place depends. Where the proportional costs are the same, there is no motive for exchange, and it is by the amount of their difference that the benefit, and therefore to a great degree the volume, of the transactions will be settled. To get a clearer perception of the real bearings of this essential condition for foreign trade let us take an actual case. What is the cause of the commerce carried on between England and the American Union, and why do certain articles form part of that commerce while others do not? Why, e.g., should not England send the wheat of its southern countries to America in exchange for the iron of Pennsylvania and the cotton goods of Massachusetts? The only explanation open is the action of the principle of comparative cost. The cost of American wheat as compared with iron in that country is lower than the cost of British wheat compared with the cost of British iron. Over the whole field of trade similar conditions operate, and it is thus that the actual ingredients of the reciprocal trade of two countries are arranged.

The action of comparative cost, using that expression with the liberal interpretation that we have put on it, as including cases of absolute limitation, is however hindered in its working. It is not, as has sometimes been said, the "sufficient condition" of foreign trade. Comparative costs of certain commodities may differ, and even differ greatly, in two countries, and yet those commodities may not be exchanged. The impelling force of all exchange is the economic motive of self-interest, and it may well happen that though the differences between the costs and therefore the values of the commodities under consideration would leave a surplus of advantage, yet the difficulties to be overcome in effecting the transfers would impose a still greater cost, and more than neutralize the gain. This kind of hindrance is present in the earliest exchanges. If tribes are divided from each other by long distances, by rivers or mountain ranges, the chances of trade are diminished, and each group is more closely confined to its own resources. What is true of primitive trade is equally applicable to the widely developed commerce of the present age. The obstacles to transport of commodities, whether natural or artificial, are even now a considerable check to international dealings in some classes of goods. In former days they practically confined foreign trade to dealings in luxuries, since none but very rare and valuable articles could bear the heavy cost of transport and the high profit which was needed as an insurance against risk. By degrees, as we saw, the expense and danger of trade have been reduced, with the result of ever increasing the list of goods that are exchanged between nations, and therefore, in Cobden's happy phrase, "widening the circle of exchanges."

Recent developments in the commerce of nations supply many illustrations ; it is as much to cheaper carriage as to virgin land that we owe the Canadian wheat trade. The American and Australian exports of meat are also in point, as is too the English export of coal that has now reached such large proportions. The German iron export may be added to the above cases ; but even the smaller industries give abundant examples, e.g. the recent increase of English fruit imports. The general principle is moreover too plain to require any lengthy elucidation or support by evidence. That the reduction of impediments will increase foreign trade is as true as that the lowering of the tolls for crossing a bridge will generally add to the traffic that passes over it.

Another agency also tends to prevent the exchange of goods between countries even where their comparative costs are not the same. Theoretical writers on political economy have often shown an unfortunate disposition to regard foreign trade as if it were in each case confined to two countries, though they would of course reject such a belief if explicitly stated. The oversight is not, however, confined to them. In popular discussion, from which all pretence of theorizing is supposed to be excluded, the same fault frequently appears. Any measure affecting trade with particular countries is estimated as if its effects were confined to such trade, and no allowance is made for the reactions that will be produced on other branches of foreign commerce. Neither in theory nor in practical questions is such an omission justifiable. Modern commerce is not confined to exchanges between any two countries, no matter how powerful or wealthy ; it is rather a system of connected markets, each of which is the seat of a smaller system. To return once more to the often-used analogy of primitive tribes or scattered settlers, we see that as the separate groups, tribes, or families become connected in the larger system of internal trade; as the settlers on a western border state come after a time to deal in the town which furnishes the traders' centre or market of their district, so do the various independent countries of the world form by degrees what we may call a world market, though it has no single locality that can be looked on as its centre. The growth of foreign commerce has made this so plain that it can hardly escape any observer's notice; but a less evident fact is that it has been gradually forming during the course of European history, and has not yet reached its limit. During the later Middle Ages the Italian cities; in the seventeenth century the Dutch; at present England; at a future time the United States, or perhaps Australasia, may claim to be the nearest approach to the central point or localization of this world market. But however this may be, the most important result for the present is, that as in the national or district market there is competition between the producers and the consumers of the various wares, so is there a like competition between the several producing and between the several consuming countries in the market of the world. The former kind of competition tends to lower the value of articles, the latter to raise it. Thus, to show the working of this state of things in fact, the competition of India, Russia, the United States, and Australia tends to lower the world value of wheat; that of India and China has a like influence on tea; while the competition of England, France, and Germany (though somewhat restricted as regards the two latter) has an opposite effect on wheat; and England, Russia, the United States, and Australia, by their competition for the supply of the tea-producing countries, raise its value. Without adding any further instances, it is apparent that the mere fact of difference in the comparative cost of wheat and iron in England and the United States will not suffice to establish an exchange of those commodities, for India may offer wheat to England on still more favourable terms, and Germany may prove a cheaper source for the iron needed by the Union. But there can be no question that the existence of each source of supply will affect the other, and that, impediments apart, there will be a movement towards a common world value for both wheat and iron. This competition of different countries, which is such a rapidly growing factor in the commerce of nations, has a profound effect on its character and conditions. It has, as we shall see, important practical bearings on questions of commercial policy, but for the moment it is chiefly interesting as marking the final step in the process of evolution by which the single and rare exchanges of savage tribes or families, which we found to be the rudimentary form of foreign trade, have passed into a world-wide system of commerce. That this development is parallel to the course of internal trade is evident, and it adds one more to the many analogies between the growth of national life and that of the body which international law describes as the family of nations. It was possible for a far-sighted person to argue from this analogy to the ultimate formation of modern international trade, and in fact the essential truth on the subject has never been better expressed than in the remarkable dictum of Dudley North, published more than two hundred years ago, which declares that " the whole world as to trade is but as one nation or people, and therein nations are as persons."

The analogy of individual exchanges at once points out the benefits that may be expected to result from those that take place between nations. As in the former class each party concerned gives what he wants less than what he receives in return, so in the course of international commerce more valuable products are obtained in exchange for less valuable ones. Looking generally at the facts, it cannot be disputed that such is the case. The corn, cotton, tea, and wine that Great Britain imports have a higher value in use to its inhabitants than the coal, iron, and manufactured goods that are exported in payment. We need only imagine the effects of a total cessation of foreign trade for six months to see the enormous advantage that is obtained through that agency, and though for other countries its absolute gain is not so great, yet in all cases there is a substantial balance of advantage. A mere general assertion of the benefits reaped through commerce is not sufficient, since in fact it is composed of distinct elements that need to be carefully indicated. The first of these particular or special gains is the supply of previously unattainable goods. The earliest commerce was directed to this object. The trader brought oriental products into countries entirely destitute of them, and manufacturers to uncivilized tribes, taking back the peculiar products of each country. Modern commerce also deals largely in such objects. A cursory examination of the articles that enter into the world's trade will establish the fact. The modern breakfast-table would be otherwise impossible, and what is true of the most civilized nations is equally true of the rudest ones. But a second result of international trade is perhaps even more advantageous. As domestic exchange enables division of employments to be carried out with an accompanying increase of production and immense gain to the community, so does the system of trade between countries allow each to develop its special aptitudes, and thereby to add in a greater degree to the wealth of the world. The territorial division of industry under which goods are produced, not only by the fittest men but in the fittest places, is an outcome of international trade, and one greatly for the material advantage of all countries. International division of labour confers a further benefit. At first it is probable that the division between individual producers was due to special qualities on the part of the workers who, so to speak, differentiated themselves from their fellows ; afterwards it is found that even were all men alike, there is a profit in assigning a special vocation to each, owing to the increased skill that practice gives. In a less degree the phenomenon repeats itself in the case of nations. The concentration of labour and capital, the superior organization of industry that is the result of directing a large part of the national production to a single object, yields a much greater return, and thereby gives a larger contribution to the total wealth of nations. It is the territorial division of labour that has placed the English cotton industry in its present position, or at least it was one of the conditions essential to its attaining that point.

For a thorough understanding of the general influence and effects that the commerce of nations is likely to produce, it is indispensable to realize clearly its connexion with the fundamental condition of division of labour and consequent specialization of employments. Unless we bring ourselves to perceive that the movement towards an increase of trade relations between nations is parallel to, and accounted for in the same way as, the growth of domestic trade, and on the whole confers the same benefits, we are likely to be mistaken both in our interpretation of the facts of foreign commerce and in our judgments on matters of commercial policy. Instances of errors produced in this way will often be met when examining legislation on the subject.

As yet but one side of the picture has been presented ; the advantages that fresh exchanges and increased division of labour bestow on society have been a favourite theme of economists, who in many cases have dwelt with peculiar satisfaction on the working of private interest for the general good. There is much justification for the course. The play of the economic organization, steadily becoming ever more and more intricate, attracted the admirer of scientific law in social matters. The immense gains to all concerned seemed the more valuable as they were obtained without any ill-judged interference on the part of the state, furnishing at once an illustration and a vindication of the working of *laissez-faire*. This mode of treatment, though tempting, had nevertheless its dangers ; if one school persistently devoted its efforts to a glorification of the results of increased exchange either internal or foreign, it was but a question of time for an opposing one to come forward which would seek to depreciate those gains and magnify any observable faults. The task of contradiction was taken up in regard to internal trade by the socialists, while the protectionists discharged a like function for foreign trade. One of the main links between these seemingly different sections is their position on the point before us. Without at present entering into the details of a controversy that will be better discussed later on, it is in place to note the portion of truth contained in the criticism of international division of labour. There can be little doubt that the more elaborate the machinery of trade the easier it is to put it out of gear. In the simple cases in which we found the origin of foreign trade a temporary disturbance did not so much matter. Each small society was in essentials self-sufficing. The intermediate stages of growth show, if not the same independence, at least considerable capacity for meeting all wants, if it should be necessary, from the national resources. The modern state is quite differently situated. Before the Great War it required a violent effort of imagination to conceive the condition of a modern European country completely isolated from all other countries. Since 1914 the social and economic difficulties experienced by Germany and Austria, in consequence of the blockade (though they were never completely isolated), and the similar difficulties experienced by Soviet Russia (though perhaps Russia is less dependent than any other great area with the possible exception of the United States on its foreign trade) since the revolution have illustrated the advantages of foreign trade in a manner which even the least thoughtful have been able to appreciate.

There is a further and perhaps on the whole a greater difficulty. The adjustment of supply and demand is always a problem that tries the skill of producers and dealers, but in regard to international commerce the task is peculiarly arduous. The regulation of supply for distant markets, the attempt to estimate what may be expected from other countries, the effect of the cross relations of the many trading nations, are all questions that, if they had to be determined by calculation, might at once be surrendered as hopeless. In spite of the wonderful acuteness which has been developed in traders through experience, mistakes often occur, and the consequence is sometimes the disastrous event known as a commercial crisis. Now if the growth of international trade has established these relations, it is evident that any loss so produced must be placed to its account.

Another drawback to division of labour has been frequently urged against the form of it in which we are specially interested. The individual workman, by being limited to a single employment, is weakened in his general powers. Some simple manual operation repeated incessantly for

2

several hours of the working day does not afford sufficient scope for the exercise of the faculties required from the citizens of a free community. There is an admitted necessity for remedying this evil by the aid of education and political training. Precisely the same evil results, it is urged, follow from unrestricted foreign trade. The nation given up to a single industry, or set of industries, may indeed, economically speaking, gain, but only at the expense of the qualities that contribute most efficiently to a vigorous national life. The best mode of dealing with such difficulties is not to ignore them or treat them with contempt ; it is rather to assign them their proper place in relation to the theory and policy of commerce. International, like all division of employments, has certain drawbacks which in striking a balance of the sum of gain should be carefully estimated. On the whole it appears that the benefits exceed by far the losses in either case. Just as no one seriously proposes to go back to the ruder systems of industrial organization because labourers are often out of employment, or some men suffer from the undue monotony of their work, so there is no valid ground for opposing the development of international commerce on account of possible wars, occasional commercial crises, or such an unhappy and one-sided form of industry as formerly prevailed in the southern states of the American Union. All these cases suggest not limitation, but further expansion and better organization of the system of exchanges, by which their evil effects will be diminished, and it may be hoped finally disappear.

In addition to the difficulties just examined, which are common to all exchange, foreign commerce has one that is peculiar to itself. When in the course of domestic trade two persons exchange goods, we may fairly assume that each is benefited, as otherwise he would not be a consenting party to the transaction. On passing to foreign trade a new complication comes in ; as before, the parties directly concerned are individuals, and we can continue to believe that they are gainers, but does it follow that the nations to which they belong also gain ? Is there not a tacit assumption that individual and national gain are identical, or in other words that there is a harmony of interests, without adequate proof of the fact ? There can be no doubt that in such cases a divergence of interests is possible—and it may be remarked that some domestic exchanges may conceivably injure the national interest ; but at the same time the gain of the individual exchanger is so far a national gain, and the increase of utility through each separate transaction of foreign trade when summed up gives the result of the whole, subject to any special losses to other members of the nations. The latter have moreover to be proved, not by vague general assertion, but by precise evidence, and it must be shown that they exceed the direct gain of exchange. Some of the most unfortunate legislative measures, e.g. the prohibition of the export of English wool in the last century, have been based on the supposed opposition between personal and national advantage, and it may safely be said that no claim should be more jealously scrutinized on its merits.

To sum up the results that we have attained—It appears that international trade in its most general form of dealings between distinct groups is of great antiquity ; that international trade is the result of differences in comparative cost of producing the articles traded in, though the action of this law is limited by hindrances to trade and the competition of different countries ; that a country derives great advantages from its foreign trade, which is from one point of view a development of the division of employments, that is at once a cause and an index of civilization ; and finally, that these gains may possibly be accompanied by certain losses, as is the case in all such division, but that these instances are merely possibilities, and not likely to be serious in practice.

CHAPTER III

MONEY AND INDEBTEDNESS IN FOREIGN COMMERCE

THE leading features of international commerce and the conditions that govern it have now been sketched. Without entering into details that are only fitted for an economic text-book it is difficult to obviate all objections, but the central position that all exchange, foreign or domestic, is usually beneficial to the persons trading, requires rather clear exposition than elaborate proof, and will receive additional support from the evidence that the actual operation of a liberal policy affords. There are, however, some questions connected with the general character of foreign trade that must be briefly examined before passing to the more practical part of our subject.

First amongst such points is the relative amount of benefit gained by trading countries. In the older theories this was a vital matter ; with some countries trade was, it was thought, always gainful, with others it was always injurious, while with a third it was good or bad according to circumstances, the one criterion of merit being the tendency to cause an influx of the precious metals. It is only necessary to glance over the titles of the chapters of Sir J. Steuart's *Principles of Political Economy* (1766) to see how completely an acute and in many respects original thinker could be led astray by the prevailing belief. The regulations of commerce, of which the eighteenth century was so full, all depended on this belief, and were directed to secure a favourable result from trade with other countries. The modern view, which regards trade as being always advantageous and benefiting both sides, and which is in general so undeniably true, places the subject in quite another light. Instead of guarding ourselves against loss, we have only to consider what is our proportion of gain, which is after all more a question of scientific curiosity than of practical importance. If it were possible by legislation to obtain a larger share of the total advantage there would be more reason for the inquiry, but, as will appear in examining the protectionist policy, any effort of the kind is not likely to succeed.

As regards the theoretical solution of the question, which forms a long and very difficult chapter in works devoted to the subject, we need only notice the chief results. In order that trade shall be steadily carried on between two countries, the value of imports must (other relations being for the moment excluded) equal the exports, since the latter are the payment for the former. This proposition is simply the extension to the sum of foreign trade of what is plainly true with regard to any particular case of barter, and cannot be denied by anyone who comprehends the real nature of trade. The establishment of this equality of value between imports and exports is brought about through the arrangement of the terms of exchange for goods, and those terms are influenced by the desires of consumers in the trading countries. Thus the more eager the demand of a country for foreign goods, the greater will be the amount of home products to be given in exchange ; and the more other countries require the products of a particular nation the better will be the terms that it can make with them. This general statement is, however, too vague to be of much practical use, and is further complicated by the existence of numerous countries which supply and demand the several products. Fortunately for the more pressing questions of policy no precise and definite solution is required, and further discussion of the matter may without loss be left to theoretical students.

A point of much greater importance, and one which has given rise to serious misconceptions of the real nature of international commerce, is that of the action of money. All modern trade is carried on by the use of a circulating medium, transactions being invariably expressed in terms of it. The exporter does not expect *goods* in exchange for what he sends out ; it is their *price* that he requires. The result is that all foreign trade is in appearance dependent

on the conditions of price, or in other words, the value of
money, and it seems as if the most essential part of trade
was that directly relative to this universally needed object.
Here, too, a reference to the case of domestic trade helps to
explain the true position. Money is an invaluable instrument for facilitating internal trade, but it is evidently not
the motive power which causes exchange. Relative prices
of goods are adjusted to their relative values, which generally depend on the cost involved in producing them.
Foreign trade is not in this respect different ; in fact where
two trading countries possess different currencies (as where
one has a gold standard, the other using inconvertible
paper money), there is little difficulty in seeing that the
trade between them is barter. The development of commerce has also helped to make the truth plainer. In the
earliest stages, before money had come into existence, no
one could think that trade was other than it appeared to be,
viz. an interchange of goods. The introduction of money
with its great advantages, and backed up by the power of
the state, led to an almost superstitious veneration for it as
the "oil," the "life blood," or the "sinews" of trade,
according to the particular line of metaphor adopted. By
the growth of the credit system, on which both domestic
and foreign trade are now based, the fact that goods are
ultimately exchanged for goods is brought home to all
concerned. Credit documents, either cheques or bills
of exchange, bear on their face their true character
and function as a part of the mechanism of exchange, as
does also the latest development in this direction—the
telegraphic transfer. The immense extent of foreign
commerce, too, goes far to disprove the notion that the
small store of money applied by nations to facilitating payments of balances in this department of trade could be the
primary force in operation.

The principal difficulty of this part of the subject is not
yet disposed of. "That in the long run goods are
for goods" ; "that the commerce of nations is in reality
a system of barter on a magnificent scale" ; and "that
money is simply an instrument to aid that barter," are
propositions of unquestionable truth ; but it is possible to

admit their correctness and yet to feel puzzled as to the operation of money on trade. " If," it may be asked, " money is nothing but a particular kind of machinery which produces no original effect, how do you explain the importance ascribed to it in the commercial world ? " " Can anyone doubt that the quantity of money in a country affects its foreign trade ? " Such questions touch the point that misleads many persons interested in the subject, and properly answered they help to dissipate mistaken views. The policy of governments during the Great War, in limiting as far as possible the export of the stock of coined metal at their disposal, has done a good deal in recent times in increasing confusion on the relationship between money and foreign trade. But the true solution is not difficult. It is a well-known fact that the precious metals are not found in large quantities except in a few places, so that the actual distribution of these metals all over the world must in itself have been the result of previous trading. But, in fact, so long as the world, or a great part of it, uses the precious metals as the basis of its currency, the distribution of that portion of the total supply which *is* used as currency is in itself determined by the trade of the world. So long as the movement of the metals is free any excess in one place is transferred to another, owing to the fact that its relative redundancy in one place raises prices there, and so makes gold or silver, or both, relatively cheap. From the standpoint of international trade, gold and silver are commodities like corn and meat and their movements are determined by causes similar to the causes which determine the movement of other articles. It is true that obstacles are often put in the way of the free movement of the metals, just as obstacles are put in the way of the free movement of other articles, with bad results in both cases ; but the fact that the primitive veneration for the precious metals which still survives in certain quarters influences the policy of governments does not elevate them into anything more than useful agents in the total processes which underlie international trade. It is true that movements in the metallic stock may influence the policies of banks, and so alter the current price of bank credit. From this point of view the attention which is paid to these movements is perfectly justified. But this is not the same thing as asserting that money is in any way the real basis of international trade.

The strongest evidence in support of this view is obtained from those cases that at first sight seem to be altogether outside it. Every one is aware that the money standards of all countries are not the same ; some use gold, others silver, and a third class put up with unconvertible paper for their circulating medium. Now with different materials for money there can be no effective redistribution of the supply. Indian silver is not available as money in England, nor English paper money in the United States, nor would the paper of the German Republic be accepted in either. Another way of reaching the same final result is adopted. Instead of sending money from England to America, or vice versa, the gold price of Fnglish Treasury Notes is altered, and has just the same effect. Instead of an automatic adjustment of the price-levels produced by movements in the metals, there is an adjustment of the price-levels brought about by the variations of the rates of exchange.

The full understanding of the proposition that all commerce is in essence the interchange of commodities, and its application to the interpretation of the movements of trade, goes a long way towards removing the difficulties that would otherwise present themselves, but it does not account for all the forms of international commercial relations. If foreign trade were merely a highly developed system of barter it would necessarily follow that the values exchanged on each side should be equal. What a country like England sends out should exactly balance what she gets in ; that is to say, imports should be equal in value to exports. This, however, is manifestly not the case either as respects English trade with any particular country, say France, or with the world at large. On the contrary, the permanent excess of imports over exports is a perpetual sorrow to the upholders of " fair-trade " doctrines, who point to it as a sufficient proof of the error of our present policy.

The difficulty finds its solution in a fuller analysis of the economic relations of nations, which are not limited to a short interval of time, and include more than the actual interchange of goods. First as regards trade with any particular country, it is evident that with the close connexion of nations that now exists, there are abundant facilities for setting off an excess of imports from one country against an excess of exports to another. England may import from America more than she exports to it, but if her exports to a third country, say India, exceed her imports thence by an equal amount, while American imports from India are greater than the exports to that country to a like amount, then by a simple balancing of accounts all liabilities can be cleared off. The realities of commerce are not so simple as the supposed case, but however many be the countries engaged, so far as the system of set-off can be used, we may be sure that it will be. Just as the clearing-house cancels an enormous number of domestic trade transactions, so does the international organization of the foreign exchanges wipe off the balances of trade between countries to the utmost extent possible. A country whose total imports and exports balance can close its accounts without difficulty.

Where, however, there is an excess of imports or of exports on the whole result of foreign commerce, this explanation does not avail. It will not account for the fact that for considerably more than half a century the imports of the United Kingdom have in every year been more than its exports. Through all the fluctuations of industry and trade, alike in times of prosperity as of adversity, this constant relation has shown itself. The difference is not indeed the same, nor even in proportion to the mass of trade ; even in the years 1902–1913 the excess raised from £183,000,000 in 1903 to as little as £124,000,000 in 1911 ; in 1859 the excess was only £24,000,000, whilst it swelled to £142,000,000 in 1877 ; but the long continuance and the vast amount of the balances, which for the forty years (1856–1895) were over £3,300,000,000, and amounted to over £1,440,000,000 for the last ten years before the outbreak of the Great War at once suggest that they are the outcome of the permanent conditions of British commerce. No explanation that refers to temporary causes or the fluctuations of trade is sufficient. Nor can the existence of the relation affect industrial welfare. No connexion between specially large excesses of imports and industrial depression can be shown. When once we see that the phenomenon is a long-continuing one, it is not difficult to obtain a satisfactory explanation of it. Besides the usual commercial interchange between countries, there are many forms of economic relations, and it is to these additional influences that the peculiarity of English trade returns is due. Exports obviously pay for imports so far as they go, but for the amount that remains other modes of discharging indebtedness must be established. Such are, first, the credit relations of the countries. Nations, or rather the individual members of nations, lend large sums to foreign governments, companies, and individuals, and these loans affect the relations of imports and exports, but in a somewhat complicated way, for the contracting of a loan increases the export from the lending country ; we may almost say the increased export *is* the loan. When an Australian state borrows in England for railway construction, and imports steel rails, railway-engines, wagons, and labourer's clothes from the same source, these forms of capital are really the shape in which the loan passes. It may be that instead of importing manufactures the colony retains so much of its products for home use ; in either case the result is the same. The relation of the two countries is affected by the contracting of the debt just as it would be if the borrowing colony had exported commodities to the same amount. The loan is practically an immaterial export. This however is but the initial effect. Borrowing under modern conditions implies the payment of interest, and consequently in succeeding years the colony of our supposition will have to meet this new liability by sending out additional exports sufficient to provide for the interest falling due ; and finally when, if ever, the principal is being refunded, it must be in the same way ; as borrowing means *pro tanto* increased imports, so does repayment mean increased exports.

The excess of English imports is largely due to the action of these agencies. The accumulated wealth of the United Kingdom for many years before the war flowed over into foreign investments, and for the time increased its exports ; by degrees the interest on the capital thus applied has grown to an even larger amount than the fresh annual supplies, with the necessary result that imports have been increased, and any check to the course of new foreign investments has at once made their excess much larger. The increase in the balance between 1872 and 1880 was for the most part due to the indisposition of English capitalists to invest in foreign securities with the freedom that they had previously done. The difference which in 1872 had been £40,000,000, rose to £125,000,000 in 1880, giving evidence of the vast extent of the international movement of capital. During the war this country borrowed largely in the United States and elsewhere, and also sold some part of its vast holdings of foreign securities. These loans and sales had the direct effect of stimulating imports. On the other hand, this country also lent large sums to its Allies and in so far as they took payment in British-made goods this lending increased exports. But much of what we bought in America with the proceeds of loans and sales never appeared in our statistics at all, being sent to France and elsewhere. The income from investments, which was estimated to be £200,000,000 in 1913 has now fallen to £120,000,000. Again, we are entitled to interest on our loans to Allies and also to reparations payments, whilst in turn we owe America for interest. If all these payments are made the explanation of the balance will be even more complicated than it now is.

The effects of borrowing, both immediate and ultimate, though very important, are not the only influences that affect foreign commerce. The actual transfer of commodities from country to country is itself a considerable industry, employing much capital and labour, and requiring for its permanent existence a reward given by the profits and wages earned. This gain evidently accrues to the countries whose citizens own and work the shipping engaged in the trade, and who furnish a kind of export in the form of services rendered. A nation that possesses a share of the carrying trade of the world will so far have an excess of imports, which are the payment for work done in this direction. The supremacy of England in shipping is therefore a second reason for her apparently excessive imports. Estimates will naturally differ as to the proper sum to assign to this cause, and post-war figures are not only affected by conditions of boom and depression, but also by alterations in the value of money. A recent careful investigation estimated the earnings of shipping at £100,000,000 in 1913 and £340,000,000 in 1920. In the case of this country we must further take into account the enormous volume of services connected with the financing of current international trade. London, as the greatest banking centre of the world, is entitled to an annual payment of many millions, estimated at some £50,000,000 in 1920, compared with £30,000,000 in 1913.

Besides these two specially powerful influences, there are several other circumstances that affect the course of foreign commerce, and help to form the total of what may be described as international indebtedness. Amongst them are—remittances to absentees ; Government payments abroad ; earnings of foreigners who remit them home. Each of these has its opposite aspects according as we consider the paying or the receiving country, but all, so far as they are operative, must be taken into account. As examples we may give the outlay of Americans in Europe, the so-called home payments of the Indian Government, and the gains of English traders and professional men resident in other countries.

It ought now to be evident that the mere imports and exports of a country are not by any means the only conditions that determine its position and economic relations with regard to other countries. They are but one element in the larger account made up by the various causes of indebtedness, and which must all be noticed in order to interpret completely the course of foreign trade. This has been already shown in respect to England, and similar considerations are applicable to other countries. It is only by taking this wider view that the large excess of

American exports can be understood ; when so regarded it becomes quite intelligible.

The recognition of the several forms of international obligation also allows of a better statement of the stable condition of trade. So long as actual exchanges only are taken into account the outgoings must, it would appear, equal the incomings in value. The true criterion of stable trade is, we now see, the equalization not of exchanges, but of all claims on each side. The debts of a nation to other nations must be balanced by the debts of other nations to it, and this point is in fact attained ; any temporary deviation during a given period being easily corrected by the passage of bullion or international Stock Exchange securities or increased exports of concrete goods from the country in debt, or by formation of an additional claim on the part of the creditor country.

The actual processes of international commerce and the refined mechanism by which accounts are adjusted, and the transfer of the precious metals as far as possible avoided, are a special part of the subject, and they illustrate the working of the general principles ; but there is no necessity for entering more fully on the details of such operations, which more fitly belong to technical treatises. A clear perception of the broad features of commerce between nations and its effects on national advantage is an absolutely requisite preliminary to any attempt to judge the merits of different lines of policy. Until we know what commerce does, and its bearing on national welfare, we cannot say whether it is wise or the reverse to prohibit it altogether, or to load it with restraints, but discussions of the technicalities of the subject may be dispensed with.

CHAPTER IV

THE MERCANTILE SYSTEM

THE real meaning and bearing of the policy known under the name of the mercantile system has been so often misunderstood, and the tendencies which produced it are so various and in appearance divergent, that some attention is needed in order to get a precise conception of its nature and working. Historians of commerce and political economy have too often looked on all systems of regulation as identical, and have therefore failed to appreciate the shades of difference in the methods employed.

The mercantile system was a natural product of the time in which it originated, and is best understood by reference to the circumstances then existing. The nations of Europe had acquired their separate national characters, and in the case of some of the most important, their distinct governments. The New World had supplied a very large addition to the stock of the precious metals, and had thus aided in breaking up the older economic system; money was more used in ordinary transactions, and was more eagerly desired by statesmen. The extensive fields of colonization offered to the maritime nations of Europe became the object of competition, partly as a means of gaining the gold and silver deemed essential for national prosperity, but partly also as furnishing at once a supply of raw materials and a market for manufacturers. The promotion of foreign commerce was seen to be powerfully assisted by the possession of a national marine that carried forth the products of the country and earned a profit for its owners. These circumstances would not of themselves fully account for the mercantile system. We must further take into account the hostilities in which the states of Europe had been engaged, which made it almost inevitable to extend the sentiments of rivalry generated by war to commercial relations. The object of the statesman was to protect the home market against the inroads of alien goods, and at the same time to develop foreign markets for home productions. In this way the store of money would be increased, and the prosperity of the nation augmented. For, even in its highest form, the mercantile school carried on that exaggerated belief in the benefits of money that has been already noticed as existing in earlier times. It did not indeed hold that money alone was wealth, but it regarded the precious metals as being a peculiarly durable and permanent form of wealth ; and besides, it accepted the view, often maintained at present, that increased supplies of money acted as a stimulus to trade. The chief advance in the later mercantile system was in respect to the methods adopted for securing the influx of this precious agent. Instead of the old regulations forbidding the export of the precious metals and providing for supervision of foreigners who might remove the national currency, it directed attention to the relation of imports and exports. When a country exported more than it imported there must be, it was argued, a debt due to it for the balance, and a debt that could be discharged only by the payment of money ; if imports were unfortunately greater than exports, the case was reversed, and the country would have to send its money abroad. To preserve the nation from loss the best way was, apparently, to take care that there should be a permanent excess of exports over imports. This object was the real point towards which all the mercantilist regulations were directed, and they can be fully understood only by reference to it. A theory of commerce was built up from a particular and inaccurate interpretation of facts, and derived its force and influence from the surrounding historical conditions and modes of thought.

The true meaning of the system comes out with greater plainness from a brief consideration of its particular methods. A whole book of the celebrated work that overthrew the system as a theoretical explanation of trade is devoted to an estimate of the actual effects of these regulations, which appear in a very different light from that in which they were viewed by their advocates. Foremost among the measures whose wisdom seemed almost self-evident to the statesmen of the seventeenth century, was the discouragement of the import of any goods that could be produced at home. It is not difficult to trace the process of reasoning by which the conclusion was reached. Every import implies a corresponding debt in money ; now, if the need of importing can be obviated, the liability will cease, but the fact that commodities can be produced in the country shows that their importation is not necessary, and therefore to hinder this needless process will so far reduce the money due to other countries and increase the national wealth. The commercial legislation of the period supplies innumerable illustrations of the use of such restrictions. Thus the French minister Colbert, who may be regarded as the greatest practical exponent of mercantilism, sought most strenuously to encourage French manufacturers by duties imposed on foreign goods. The edict of 1664, and still more that of 1667, tended strongly in this direction, and they were maintained and even increased in stringency by later enactments. So in England all competition with the native woollen manufacture was impeded as much as possible. The silk and iron industries received the same aid and by degrees most of the smaller manufactures obtained some measure in their favour. In fact, this most important of the mercantile expedients has passed on to modern protectionism, where we shall again meet it.

Another part of the system has not had equal vitality, viz. that which aimed at prohibiting trade of any description whatsoever with certain countries. The great object of trade being the obtaining of the precious metals, through the maintenance of a " favourable " balance—i.e. an excess of exports over imports—it seemed advisable to hinder any part of it that was not likely to produce this result. The trade with France was regarded with disapproval by the English mercantile writers, since the French wines and other luxuries would not in any way contribute to the accumulation of wealth, while the English " thrifty " and durable goods would aid the French in some degree in securing a further gain. Moreover, trade with any country with which there was an unfavourable balance was for the time looked on as undesirable. The legislator was bound to watch carefully the movements of imports and exports with each country, and to regulate his policy according to their fluctuations.

The diminution of imports is one very obvious way of acting on the " balance of trade." Another, and equally effective one, is the increase of exports. For this end the machinery of drawbacks and bounties was brought into play. Duties on imported articles were taken off, or, as it was said, " drawn back," when they were re-exported, and special branches of domestic production received premiums or bounties on the amount of their exports. Though there is a clear distinction between the mere refunding of duties and the payment of actual rewards for exportation, yet, in fact, the two were mixed up, bounties being often disguised under the cover of repayment of duty—a course not unknown in modern times. Both had so far the same effect on the balance of trade ; they, it was believed, helped to make it favourable, and both were for this reason favoured by the mercantile school.

As the experience of commercial facts grew larger, it was discovered that the course of trade was not quite so simple and uniform as had been supposed. What at first seemed evil might yield future advantages. This explains some parts of the mercantile regulations that are in apparent contradiction to the general aim of increasing exports of goods. Export duties, or—as in the case of English wool—absolute prohibition of export, were placed on raw materials of manufacture. The immediate gain by export was lost, but was compensated by the expectation of the greater ultimate advantage from the export of the manufactured product. English wool, if retained at home, could at a later time be exported in the more valuable form of woollen manufactures. The preservation of native raw materials for the use of manufacturing industry was an essential part of the mercantile doctrine.

The position of the nations of Europe, and their relations with the New World, were the cause of further developments of the policy. The difference of trade with different

3

countries led to active endeavours to encourage it with some and to hinder it with others. The apparatus of duties might suffice for the latter, but a treaty of commerce was the favourite device for the former. Where a country was likely to supply raw materials that could be worked up and then exported, or, better still, possessed a superabundance of gold, and silver she was induced to trade by the offer of special advantages. Thus Russian trade was sought for, as giving a plentiful supply of materials for ships ; and Portugal received advantages for her wines, as against those of France, by the famous Methuen Treaty (1703), on account of her command of the mines of Brazil.

A still more remarkable aspect of mercantilism is found in its colonial policy. The acquisition of possessions in other continents had powerfully affected European countries, each of which naturally desired to make the utmost profit out of these fresh openings. Politically, the colony was dependent on the mother-state, and this subjection was turned into a system of " exploitation." The colony was to supply suitable raw materials for the trade, and a market for the manufactures, of its proprietor. The worst features of the mercantile system appear in the treatment of colonies and dependencies. Their trade with other countries was placed under severe restrictions, the great object being to secure a sole market for the goods of the metropolitan state. Colonial products had to pass through the home market, where they were either worked up into higher forms, or directly exported to foreign countries. Spain, France, Holland, Portugal, and England all pursued this method of colonial management, though with different degrees of severity, till the overthrow of the system.

Besides the direct import and export of commodities, the shipping employed in the transport of goods is an important commercial item, and the mercantile system prescribed the encouragement of this branch of native industry. Whichever of two countries possessed the carrying trade between those countries would gain on the balance of trade, since, in addition to her ordinary exports, she would have to be paid for freights earned by her ships. Hence the " Navigation Acts " employed both by England and

France as a means of transferring the Dutch shipping business to themselves.

Such were the main features of the mercantile policy as it appeared in its full development. It is impossible to dwell at any length on each of the parts of the system, which naturally varied in different countries, but this makes it all the more necessary to remark that any attempt to give very briefly its broad aspects prevents our noticing the limitations and modifications that existed both in theory and practice. Writers who are classed as mercantilists form very divergent estimates of the value of the precious metals ; of the importance of national industry ; and of shipping or the colonial trade. So, too, the differences in practical legislation were by no means insignificant. Colbert is usually taken as a type of mercantile statesmanship, but his earlier measures show great moderation in the imposition of duties, while his testimony as to the temporary nature of the policy is on record. In truth, the mercantile is like the feudal system, rather a phase in the historical evolution of Europe than a symmetrical body of doctrine applied everywhere with equal rigour. There is, nevertheless, the utmost necessity for understanding its position and methods. Without exaggeration we may say that most of modern protectionism is simply a representation of the policy of the mercantile school with some of the leading conceptions modified and adjusted to meet the altered circumstances of the present. Restraint of importation is an aim common to both, and even the reasons assigned do not differ much ; the method of bounties is in operation in some noticeable cases, and fragments of the colonial policy survive in the French colonies. The traditions of the system have further helped to create one very important part of protectionism, but as it were by repulsion. American followers of Carey accept their master's view that " the American system," as they style protection, is necessary to counteract the baneful action of the English colonial policy of the eighteenth century. In these various ways mercantilism has so affected the course of economic history and policy as to need notice in considering the problems of to-day.

An estimate of the economic and social effects of the mercantile system is not quite so easy to form, and the vacillations of opinion in this respect have been remarkable. At first it was regarded as a masterpiece of wisdom and state-craft. Then, under the influence of the liberalizing movement of the eighteenth century, it was condemned as a gigantic imposture. Quesnay, the founder of the French school of *Économistes*, has pronounced a memorable condemnation of the system of Colbert, who, "intoxicated by the trade of Holland and the *éclat* of manufactures of luxuries, threw his country into such madness that people no longer speak of anything except trade and money, without considering the proper use of money or the real trade of a country." Adam Smith's abhorrence of the "mean and malignant" expedients of the mercantile system is shown all through the *Wealth of Nations*, and the followers of these distinguished economists have adopted their judgment. Fuller historical inquiry, and the general change in the attitude of economists, have led to a more sympathetic treatment of the older policy. Many modern students think with Roscher that a system which has lasted for centuries cannot be wholly erroneous, and they notice that the direction in which the mercantile policy tended to guide society was the true line of progress. The development of manufactures and the organization of national economies with varieties of industrial pursuit were essential for the growth of the European state system. They thus reach the conclusion that mercantilism was a necessary and beneficial stage of social development, not to be contemptuously set aside as the product of error and selfishness. There is much in this view that is in harmony with modern thought, but it needs certain corrections before being accepted. The conditions that produced the mercantile policy have been already set forth, and it is plain that they naturally led to its adoption. Its beneficial action is not so clearly made out. The time had not come for widely extended trade; international relations were in too rudimentary a condition to allow of active commerce, but the hindrances on such commercial intercourse as actually existed were, we believe, extremely detrimental to progress.

It was perhaps as impossible for the men of that time to understand this fact as to disbelieve in witchcraft. We cannot, however, doubt that a wider insight would have been for the advantage of national life.

CHAPTER V

THE OVERTHROW OF THE MERCANTILE SYSTEM—TRANSITION TO PROTECTION

THE system of policy sketched in the preceding chapter reached its full development about the middle of the eighteenth century. In every part of commercial legislation its principles were predominant, and had come to be regarded by practical men as unquestionable. Symptoms of dissatisfaction had, indeed, previously manifested themselves. Both in England and France such writers as Dudley North and Boisguillebert had dissented from the efforts to encourage manufactures, and the former had insisted on the value of freedom in industrial matters. But now the opposition became more serious. The French *Économistes* laid down the doctrine of absolute liberty in the most uncompromising form. " Maintain complete liberty of commerce," said their leader Quesnay ; " for the regulation of internal and external commerce that is most certain, most precise, and most profitable to the nation and to the state, consists in full liberty of competition." This general rule enunciated in different ways and expanded into volumes, formed the substance of their teaching.

Adam Smith took the same line, and stated forcibly the advantages of the " simple and obvious system of natural liberty," whereby " all systems of preference or restraint " were taken away. His arguments have passed into the substance of economic teaching, and do not require restatement here, but two common misapprehensions on the subject ought to be noticed, as they both tend to obscure the real nature of the movement and the agency that produced it.

Thus it is very commonly thought that the revolt against mercantilism was the outcome of speculation by students of

social matters—a contest of " theory " against " practice."
The persistence of this belief is noteworthy, as it has had
important effects on the progress of the later free-trade
movement.   The foundation for it is very slight.   The first
persons to feel acutely the pressure of restrictions were
those actually engaged in commerce, and it appears from
the " *mémoires* " of the representatives of the principal
commercial towns of France (prepared in 1701) that they
were in favour of freedom of commerce subject to moderate
duties.   One of them asserts that " a manufacture that
cannot be established or maintained with a duty of 12%
to 15% should be regarded in the same light as a man who
seeks to enrich himself at the public expense."   Commerce
is declared to be appointed for the supply of reciprocal
wants, and to seek to do without it is to go " against nature
and the decrees of Providence."   These sentiments would
not be out of place in much later times, and they make
the direction of wiser commercial opinion.   In Scotland
the merchants of Glasgow had among them advocates of
freedom of commerce, who confirmed Adam Smith in his
opinions.   The evils of a rigorous system of restrictions on
trade are necessarily first perceived by those who suffer
from it, though they may not formulate their objections in
the shape of a general theory.   The influence of actual
conditions on the economic doctrines prevailing at a given
time is now a commonplace of the historians of Political
Economy.   As the doctrine of free commerce seems to
have arisen from practical needs, so was it supported by
appeals to experience.   Each part of the mercantile system
was assailed by Adam Smith, not so much for its infringe-
ment of natural liberty as for its prejudicial effect on the
" progress of opulence," or, as we should say, on the
" increase of wealth."   To limit importation was contrary
to the interests of the community ; to prohibit the export of
raw materials or machinery was an injury to the particular
producers engaged in those industries.   Restrictions on
colonial trade retarded the growth of these young societies,
while they did not benefit the parent state.

Another error on the subject is even more common.   It
consists in the belief that the free-trade policy was

universally, or to a great extent, triumphant; that *laissez-faire* became an established rule. So far is this from being the case that the system of restriction has never been entirely abandoned. Its theoretical basis has in outward appearance been changed, but at no time has there been the complete victory of free trade which is sometimes imagined. When tracing the history of the different tariffs, we shall see how persistent, under one form or another, has been what is now known as " protection."

The movement of the eighteenth century was nevertheless a liberalizing one ; its very failures were the ground on which later and more successful efforts were built. Though most of the reforms in economic legislation were in respect to industry and internal trade, there were yet some advantages gained for international commerce. The revolt of the American colonies of England destroyed at a blow one part of the English mercantile system, and showed on how weak a basis it rested. Another of the expedients denounced by Adam Smith—the negotiation of commercial treaties with the object of securing special advantages for the bargaining parties—was employed for a different and wiser purpose, viz. to remove or relax the barriers created by prohibitions and high duties between nations. The period 1780–1790 is remarkable for the number of these engagements. The United States commenced their national career by seeking to form liberal treaties with European countries. The first was with France in 1778 ; and after the recognition of their independence by England, they were willing to form a similar agreement with her. More remarkable still was the once famous Eden treaty (1786) between France and England. The sharpest weapons of the restrictive system had been reserved by each of these nations for the other. " Our jealousy and our hatred of France," said Hume, " are without bounds. . . . These passions have created innumerable barriers and obstructions upon commerce, while we are accused of being commonly the aggressors." It has been already mentioned (p. 32) that the trade with France had been declared a nuisance, and the attempt to arrange a commercial treaty after the Peace of Utrecht (1713) had failed to receive the sanction of Parliament, owing to the popular opposition it excited. Such trade as existed between the two countries was carried on by smugglers, who distributed the silks, wines, and brandies of France in spite of the penalties established by legislation on the subject. The Peace of Versailles (1783) was accompanied by a stipulation for a commercial treaty, but great difficulty was experienced in getting the governments to carry out this provision by appointing commissioners for the purpose of settling the new duties on the different commodities. French writers usually attribute the delays to the treachery of English statesmen, though at a later time the negotiation of the treaty was regarded as a piece of British state-craft, having for its object the destruction of French manufactures. Finally the commissioners were appointed, and succeeded in arranging a definite set of duties which, though opposed in the English Parliament by Fox and (one regrets to add) by Burke, came into force at the end of 1786.

The changes made were very important. The duty on French wines was reduced to less than one-half of the previous prohibitive rate (i.e. from £96 to £45 per tun). Brandy, vinegar, olive-oil, porcelain, glass, and the many Parisian manufactures received much more favourable terms. On the other hand, English textile goods, hardware and pottery were relieved from prohibitions, and instead subjected to moderate duties of 10%, 12%, or 15%, according to the particular articles. The only exceptions to this, for the time, very liberal arrangement were silk on the part of England, and mixtures of cotton and wool on that of France ; both these classes of goods being still prohibited.

As was hoped by the negotiators, the effect on trade was immediate. Before 1786 the English exports to France, according to French official returns, came to only thirteen million livres ; the inclusion of the contraband trade raised the total to twenty-four million livres. French exports to England were probably about the same. For the three years following the treaty the figures were as tabulated on next page.

These figures show the benefit to trade of a system of low duties, and notwithstanding the complaints of some French manufacturers, it appears that in neither country did industry as a whole suffer by the larger importations. France agreed to treaties with Holland and Russia on the same principle of generous and equal treatment. Unfortunately the period of moderation did not last long. Six

Year.	English Exports to France. *Livres.*	French Exports to England. *Livres.*
1787	49,440,000	34,200,000
1788	59,913,000	31,100,000
1789	60,912,000	35.100,000

years after its formation the Anglo-French treaty of 1786 was abrogated by war. It, however, produced some results on legislation. The general tariff, drawn up by the Constituent Assembly, though distinctly influenced by a protectionist bias, yet followed in its broad lines the regulations of the treaty ; there were some additional prohibitions (as, e.g., glass), but the scale of duties was calculated in the same way and came to about the same rate. Writing in 1852, the eminent economist, Chevalier, declared that, " Taken as a whole the conditions of the tariff of 1791 were very liberal. Anyone who compares it with that actually in force will be surprised at the enormous difference."

A similar disposition appeared in England. Pitt consolidated the customs laws, which had grown to an unwieldy size, and was credited with a plan for abolishing both customs and excise, and thus making Great Britain a " free port."

The French Revolution and the wars that arose out of it destroyed any hope of realizing these reforms. Fiscal necessities made the imposition of fresh taxation rather than the removal of that already existing the matter of most urgency. High duties were one of the chief resources of the financier, and native industries already pressed by taxation had a plausible claim for assistance against foreign competition. Besides, the natural tendency of warfare is to impede commercial intercourse, since it is illegal between belligerents, and even neutrals are subjected to more rigid supervision. These features, common to all wars, were peculiarly prominent in the period 1792–1815. No European state was able to avoid being drawn into the contest at one time or another, while the gross violations of neutral rights by both England and the French Empire forced the United States into an attitude of hostility towards the aggressors.

The roots of commercial policy lie deep in the past. Nations follow with curious persistence certain definite lines of conduct. To thoroughly comprehend the present situation, we must know the general outlines of earlier policies and of theories that are now given up ; but nevertheless there is little exaggeration in the assertion that it was in the time of transition from the last century to the present that the form of most existing tariff legislation had its origin. It was during it that "mercantilism" was transformed into "protectionism." The present is there-fore a fitting place, before considering the tariff legislation of the present century, to notice the characteristics of this revised and reorganized doctrine.

The key-note of protectionism is the appeal to *national* interest. Whatever be the special doctrines that its advocates attach to their main idea, this is always found in a claim of patriotism from an economic point of view. So far the most ardent free-trader might agree, but protec-tionism adds to the idea of national interest the further belief that there is an opposition between the interest of the nation and that of other nations. It retains the mercantile doctrine that the two parties to an exchange do not gain, or in more extreme form, " that the gain of one is the loss of another." The consonance of such a belief with the sentiments engendered by war is apparent, and in practice the advocates of protection regard commerce rather as a field of conflict than as a process of peaceful co-operation. Many of their minor dogmas, such as the " tribute imposed by a drain of gold," " the invasion of foreign goods," " the necessity of repelling attacks on national industry," betray their warlike origin by the terms in which they are stated.

As protectionism naturally arises in a period of warfare, so is it likely to be continued when that period has passed.

A protracted war is itself a species of protection in so far as it makes the obtaining of foreign commodities more difficult. Under the cover of this natural protection various industries are established which become exposed to foreign competition at the return of peace. The importance of these interests offers an inducement to the legislator to supply by high duties on their particular products the advantage they have lost through peace. We shall see the action of this force in both the French and American tariffs. The need of revenue and the demands of interested classes coincide with the sentiments created by the existence of hostilities.

To conclude : the modern protective system may be said to have its origin in the political and economic situation of the world at the commencement of the present century. In its structure three contributing elements can be traced, viz. (1) the influence of national sentiment with the concomitant dislike to other countries ; (2) the survival of the fallacies of the mercantile system in the minds of the public ; and (3) the urgency of special classes who are interested in obtaining advantages over foreign producers.

These general characteristics are noticeable, but of course in very unequal proportions, in the legislation of different nations, though they have for the greater part disappeared from that of Great Britain.

CHAPTER VI

THE ENGLISH CUSTOMS SYSTEM, 1815–1860

AT the conclusion of the Napoleonic War, the tax system of England was as severe as could well be imagined. The need of revenue had led to the imposition of high duties on most articles of consumption, and on the raw materials of industry. Foreign manufactures were in some cases prohibited, in all subjected to heavy differential duties. As long as the war continued the importation of corn was effectually checked, and at its conclusion the landed interest obtained a Corn Law far exceeding in rigour any earlier measure. Its declared aim was to fix the price of wheat at 80s. per quarter, which was then believed to be the "remunerative price" (i.e. the lowest price that would enable the British farmer to cultivate at a profit). The injustice of the distribution of taxation was increased by the rejection of the Income and Property Tax of 10% that had been established under the pressure of war. Notwithstanding the enormous public burdens, English manufactures were rapidly progressing, owing to the application of inventions and the disorganization of industry on the Continent. The so-called "Continental System" of Napoleon, which was simply a commercial war, though it caused serious fluctuations in commerce, failed in its object of crushing Great Britain. Economic forces are too powerful for the strongest despot, and England alone possessed the new implements of production that have brought about the transformation of modern industry. An elaborate contraband trade came into existence, by which manufactures were exported from England and distributed to continental consumers. The effect of the war was thus equivalent to that of a high protective tariff in England, while the foreign demand for its products was too keen to be destroyed by any hindrance.

The history of the English customs since 1815 has to describe the steps by which the network of protective duties and commercial regulations was abolished, and the policy of protection changed into one of pure free trade, or, if the term be preferred, into a " revenue system." This extraordinary transformation, as we may say from " black to white," was accomplished gradually—to carry on the parallel, a letter at a time. The study of this series of movements, besides its actual importance in connexion with the existing English policy, has a further value as indicating the course of future reform in other countries. However improbable it may at present seem that the high protective duties of foreign states should be modified into a pure revenue system, it is by no means so unlikely as any reform of the English tariff would have appeared at the conclusion of peace in 1815. To hope for the establishment of free trade in England was, in Adam Smith's opinion, Utopian ; and we may derive some confidence as to the future from the contradiction that facts have given to his belief.

The growth of the existing free-trade policy may be divided into three periods, with each of which the name of a distinguished statesman is connected. The first includes the reductions of duties and the removal of various restrictions during the years 1824–1827 ; it is naturally associated with the action of Huskisson, who was the moving spirit in those reforms. The political agitation excited by the Reform struggle and the pre-occupation of the Whig administration with other and, at the time, more pressing measures, prevented progress in commercial policy until the accession of Peel to office in 1841. The great alterations made in the protective system in 1842 and 1845, as well as the abandonment of the Corn Laws in 1846, make the second stage in the advance towards the present position, for which Peel was in a great degree responsible. Finally the full application in all its details of the principle of free commerce to the British tariff was the work of Mr. Gladstone, accomplished chiefly in 1853 and 1860. Each period has its characteristic features, but all contributed towards the final result, and all were needed under the existing conditions ; and it is probable that the prejudices of the people and the strength of the protected interests would not permit any quicker rate of progress.

The duties on both raw materials and manufactures existing in 1820 were so high as to now appear almost incredible. Thus raw silk was charged 5s. 7½d. per lb. ; wool, which had formerly been imported free, was first made subject to duty in 1803, and by 1819 the rate had risen to 6d. per lb. Timber, so important an element in the cost of building, was taxed 65s. per load, the inferior Canadian wood being admitted at the nominal rate of 2s. 6d. Salt, the basis of various chemical products, was charged 15s. per bushel ; tallow, hides, and other similar articles were taxed with equal severity. Foreign manufactures met with still worse treatment. Duties, amounting in some instances to prohibitions, and ranging from 40% to 180%, hindered the growth of imports. Sugar, the staple product of the West Indian colonies, was charged differently according to the place of production. West Indian, 30s. per cwt. ; East Indian, 37s. per cwt. ; foreign sugar, the enormous amount of 63s. per cwt. French wines and brandies, as well as tea and coffee, were all placed under heavy burdens. Wine from France was subject to 13s. 8½d. per gallon ; Peninsular wine escaped with 9s. 1½d. ; French brandy paid 22s. 6d. per gallon ; the tea duty was over 100% ; that on foreign coffee 2s. 6d. per lb. Though many of the commodities could not possibly have been produced at home, and therefore the duties on them would not at first appear to be " protective," yet, as they encouraged the employment of substitutes and in all cases checked consumption, and thereby indirectly the increase of exports, they were contrary to economical as well as fiscal policy. Besides, the colonial producers were unduly favoured, with results far from encouraging to those who would advocate a revival of the system. The duties protecting agriculture give another illustration of the general policy. The Corn Laws, with practical prohibition until the price of wheat reached 80s. per quarter, have been noticed before, but other agricultural imports were heavily taxed. Bacon, 28s. per cwt. ; butter, 20s. ; cheese, 10s. 6d. ; lard, 8s. ;

potatoes, 2s. The smallest and most insignificant articles did not escape—peas, hemp-seed, madder, are examples. The enumeration of separate instances brings home the fact of the determined application of restrictions to British trade in all its departments.

There is no exaggeration in the description given by Newmarch. " At that time (1820) the system of prohibition, protection, and fiscal confusion was at its height. It was said by competent authorities that the number of Acts of Parliament relating to the entry, export, and custody of goods as matters of Custom House supervision, was not less than fifteen hundred. All the special interests were in full possession of the vested rights to which they laid claim. There was the Corn Law of 1815 ; there were the differential duties in favour of the West India proprietors ; the monopoly of the East India Company ; the rigorous application of the Navigation Laws against competition on freights. There were heavy duties on raw materials of industry, and prohibitive or extravagant duties on foreign manufactures."

It was to be the task of enlightened statesmanship to destroy the system so described. The first impetus to reform came from the petition of the merchants of London for free trade, presented to Parliament in 1820. This remarkable document, which contains in very narrow compass a vigorous statement of the argument for free commerce, was drawn up by Mr. Tooke, and signed by several persons, who however were not fully capable of seeing its practical wisdom. The parliamentary inquiries into the position of the finances assisted in propagating more liberal ideas, and prepared the way for Huskisson's measures when he took the post of President of the Board of Trade in 1823. During each year of office he succeeded in carrying some needed reform, and many of the most important industries were affected by the new policy. The whole system previously applied to the silk trade was altered ; the duties on imported raw and thrown silk were reduced, the former first to 3d., then to 1d., per lb. ; the prohibition on imported silk manufactures was turned into an import duty of 30% ; the bounties on exportation were given up ; and the arrangement of the industry was placed on a more natural bas's.

The duty on imported wool was lowered to 1*d*. per lb., the prohibition of its export being changed into an export duty of the same amount. Another step in the direction of freedom of commerce was the removal of the duties on trade between Great Britain and Ireland, which completed the commercial union of the three kingdoms. Besides the substantive changes in the customs, a careful consolidation of the numerous and conflicting statutes was carried out, the whole unwieldy mass of rules being reduced to eleven Acts. The effect of these measures was seen in the increased consumption of commodities, while the protected industries, and particularly the silk trade, did not suffer as much as had been apprehended.

The death of Lord Liverpool and the disruption of the ministry closed this stage of commercial reform. From 1827–1842 the advance was insignificant. The Corn Laws were changed in 1828, but though the price at which free admission was allowed was somewhat lower—73*s*. per quarter—their effect was quite as mischievous as before.

Even after Huskisson's reforms, the operations of English commerce were sadly hampered by the many duties still retained. Parnell's *Financial Reform*, which acquired additional value from being the production of a statesman thoroughly familiar with the course of the commercial policy of the time, places the existing evils in a strong light. The duties on raw materials are shown to restrict several useful industries, and are declared to have the effect " of deranging the natural course in which labour and capital would be employed, productions extended, and the wealth, comforts, and enjoyments of the community increased." The prohibition to export machinery is condemned as destructive to the export trade that would certainly arise were it removed. With respect to the high taxation of such articles of general consumption as wine, tea, coffee, etc., we learn that, " as the effect of these high duties is in some cases to diminish the revenue, and in all to create smuggling, and further, by greatly diminishing the importation of the articles on which they fall, to diminish the

4

demand for and the exportation of our own manufactures, they are exceedingly injurious, and ought to be reduced." Finally, the number and pressure of the protective duties on both agriculture and manufactures are clearly brought out. Above all, the course of future fiscal reforms is indicated in the separation between the productive and non-productive taxes. Sir H. Parnell takes up the English revenue of 1829, amounting roughly to about £50,000,000. Of this amount about £6,000,000 was obtained by the objectionable duties on raw materials, £2,000,000 by the protective duties on manufactures, and about £3,000,000 by the *excessive* taxation of foreign spirits and tobacco. The remaining revenue of over £38,000,000 was levied in a fairly prudent and economical way. The removal of the former classes of duties would, he admits, leave a temporary deficiency which could be met by retrenchment of expenditure and the imposition of an income-tax, while the yield of the taxes retained would be much increased through the improvement of industry and trade. The fiscal working of Huskisson's policy had confirmed his views. "The abatement of revenue by taxes remitted would have been in 1827, as compared with 1823, no less than £9,182,571; it proved to be only £3,308,316; the difference of £5,874,255 being the increase of revenue from increased consumption." How fruitful the application of this principle has been in English finance will appear in the history of the later reforms.

It is plain that the measures of the period 1823–1827 were merely preparatory. So far as they went they gave confirmation to the theoretical arguments of free-traders by refuting the assertion that protection was needed by British industries. But the great bulk of the restrictive regulations continued in force, leaving an ample field for the profitable application of the policy so admirably and convincingly set forth by Sir H. Parnell.

The second period of reform is coincident with the administration of Peel from 1841–1846, and was, in fact, largely due to his efforts. To those whose acquaintance with the course of commercial policy is limited to the result of the Corn Law struggle, this statement may seem surprising. The services of Cobden and Villiers will occur to them as far more efficient than those of Peel, who might not unreasonably be regarded as an opponent of free commerce, converted, as statesmen too often are, by the force of necessity. Such a view is, however, superficial. The Corn Laws were undoubtedly the stronghold of the protected interests with the main props of the West India and shipping industries ; the wisest policy for the agitator was to assail the " Corn Law as," in Cobden's phrase, " the foster-parent of all other monopolies." The tax on food imposed in the interest of a wealthy class was, moreover, the most unpopular part of the system, and the one against which public opinion could be most readily excited. But to persons trained in the study of fiscal questions and disposed to weigh with care the possibilities of success in carrying legislative measures, a class to which Peel eminently belonged, the minor articles of the tariff would seem more promising objects of amendment. The system of import duties had been fully examined by a Parliamentary Committee in 1840, which collected a body of evidence that is said to have powerfully impressed Sir R. Peel. The evidence showed that 1,150 different items were enumerated in the list of dutiable goods, besides some forty coming under general heads ; that in 1838–9, 349 articles produced in the aggregate only £8,050 ; that, on the other hand, nine commodities yielded £18,575,000 out of a total slightly exceeding £22,100,000, or six-sevenths of the total receipts. For the year ending Jan. 5th, 1840, the net produce of the customs was £22,962,610. Of that amount ten commodities produced £20,871,136 ; six other commodities, £1,147,148. Thus, speaking broadly, sixteen articles contributed over £22,000,000, while all the other customs duties gave less than £1,000,000. Examined in detail many of the items yielded so little as to excite ridicule : e.g. in 1839–1840 : crystal beads, subject to 28s. 6d. per 1,000, gave 1s. 7d. revenue ; extract of vitriol, subject to 25% duty, 12s. 3d. ; starch, at a duty of £9 10s. per cwt., 1s. 9d. ; Bruges thread, charged 15s. per 12 lbs., only 1s. 3d.

The accumulation of facts of this description, set forth

gravely by skilled official witnesses and emphasized by the report of the Committee expressing "their strong conviction of the necessity of an immediate change in the import duties of the kingdom," was the immediate cause of the reform of 1842. Without touching the Corn Laws, it was possible to remove the minor duties that were the outposts of the protective system. Peel himself stated the general principles upon which he proceeded. Put shortly, they were—(1) the removal of all absolute prohibitions and the change of prohibitory duties into lower ones; (2) the reduction of duties on raw materials to a nominal amount; (3) half-manufactured articles to be admitted on payment of moderate duties; and (4) the admission of full manufactures, subject only to such duties as would allow of fair competition—e.g. generally about 20%.

The timber duty was considerably reduced, and the differential rate on foreign timber lessened; coffee was treated in like manner; and the more oppressive duties on raw materials—e.g. those on indigo and turpentine— were completely remodelled. In all 750 articles were affected by these changes. The results were found to accord with the expectations formed by the minister. There was a steady recovery in the revenue from customs, and trade improved under the stimulus of the remissions.

The success of the new policy emboldened ministers to proceed further in the same direction. In 1845 a still more radical revision of the tariff was carried out. Four hundred and fifty items disappeared altogether. Raw materials were the chief objects in this list. Among them were raw silk, hemp, cotton, hides, and most of the articles whose taxation was condemned by Parnell in 1830. The differential duties on sugar—that from slave-holding countries excepted—were diminished. Customs duties, estimated at £3,614,000, the larger part of which pertained to sugar, were surrendered by this measure. The number of heads of duties was reduced nearly one-half—from 1,150 to 590.

The steady progress in tariff reform, which we have just noticed, was overshadowed in the popular mind by the Corn Law struggle. It was useless to point out to the more advanced free-traders that substantial improvements had been made. The Corn Laws, the Navigation Acts, and the favours to colonial producers by the differential duties on sugar and timber, still remained, and it was against them that the attack was directed. How long the contest might have continued under ordinary circumstances we cannot say. The bad harvest of 1845 and the Irish Famine brought on a crisis. Peel, already convinced of the soundness in principle of free trade, and having seen the advantage of the withdrawal of protection from manufactures, recognized that the time had come for applying the sound principle without reservation to every branch of commerce. The sentiments created by the teachings of the Anti-Corn Law League completed his conversion. The practical consideration that these laws once suspended could never again be enforced in the face of the opposition, settled the question, and accordingly the Act of 1846 provided that for three years the maximum duty per quarter should be 10s., falling, as the price rose above 48s., till, at the price of 53s. per quarter, the duty would be only 4s. At the end of three years there was to be only a fixed registration duty of 1s. per quarter. The passage of this law closed the history of the protective corn duties, as, despite some feeble attempts in 1851–2, there never has been any question as to the necessity of free trade in the most essential article of food.

The fate of the Corn Laws entailed the removal of the colonial and shipping privileges. The differential duties on foreign timber had already been lowered, and in 1847–8 the rate on foreign timber was fixed at 15s., while colonial timber came in at the very low rate of 1s. But the completion of the reform was delayed. Slave-grown sugar was placed on an equality with other foreign sugar in 1846, and provision was made for equalization of the duties on all sugars to take place in 1851.

Great as was the importance of both the landed and colonial interests, the shipping industry had both historically and politically perhaps superior claims. The Navigation Laws have been traced as far back as the fourteenth century, and had been maintained continuously since 1651. As a political measure they had won the approval of Adam Smith, and had long been regarded as one essential condition of British naval supremacy.

Huskisson's reciprocity measures made the first break in the system, which was abolished in 1849 for the foreign trade and in 1854 for the coasting trade. Thus the term British ship—which had previously been conferred only on vessels built in the British Islands whose captain and three-fourths of whose crew were British subjects, and whose owner was also British—was extended to all vessels satisfying the last-mentioned condition. The completion of each of those reforms lies outside the period under notice, but important steps involving the final result were taken as regards all of them in the period 1840–1850.

The second Peel administration (1841–1846) had carried on the work begun by Huskisson: it had realized the plans of Parnell and the proposals of the Committee of 1840. It had further been forced to recognize the power of the Anti-Corn Law movement, and by the mouth of its leader had done tardy justice to Cobden and his colleagues. It is plain that the conversion to a liberal commercial policy was gradual. It was not on the authority of general principles that the reforms of 1842 and 1845 had been brought forward. One member of the Government, who was intimately acquainted with the motives of its commercial policy, and who was afterwards to carry them to their legitimate results, has placed this on record—" I am a deliberate adherent," wrote Mr. Gladstone in 1845, " of that policy which is described in contemptuous terms as halting between two opinions—between the opinion which regards commercial restriction as being permanently and essentially a good, and the opinion which deals with it as an evil necessarily greater than that of a sharp and violent transition to freedom." It is in virtue of belonging to this transitional period of commercial policy that the measures of the second stage of reform have acquired their characteristic marks.

The success of the free-trade measures, as judged by the broad test of the national prosperity that followed them, acted as an impressive object-lesson in economic practice.

Free trade passed into a maxim to be carefully observed by statesmen. Instead of cautiously feeling the way towards a system that would permit the best employment of the national resources, it became possible to boldly examine the mass of existing legislation, and to test each item by its accordance or non-accordance with the rule of free industry and trade. To make the first breach in the protective system had been Huskisson's task ; to take away the foundations of that policy by introducing a large free-trade element was the service rendered by Sir R. Peel ; to apply the new principle of legislation in its fullest extent, and to bring the still very complicated customs system into harmony with it, was the work reserved for Mr. Gladstone.

This last stage of fiscal reform was, like the second, carried out in two instalments—the first in 1853, the second in 1860. After the final defeat of the protectionists and the overthrow of the Derby ministry in 1852, Mr. Gladstone became Chancellor of the Exchequer. His first Budget speech announced " something like a new revision of the general rates," guided by the following rules : viz. (1) to abolish, unless in exceptional cases, unproductive duties ; (2) to likewise abolish duties on half-manufactured articles ; (3) to reduce duties on finished manufactures to 10%, the silk duty being exceptionally retained at 15% ; (4) to make duties specific instead of *ad valorem* ; (5) to as far as possible get rid of differential duties ; and (6) to lower duties on articles of food of general consumption.

The application of these principles freed 123 articles from duty, reduced the rates on 133 more, and besides on several minor articles of food—apples, nuts, eggs, oranges, lemons, raisins, cocoa, tea, butter, and cheese. The customs tariff became simpler and more easily understood, while finally a good many of the existing remains of protection were cleared off. The Crimean War interrupted the course of improvement, as war usually does ; seven years elapsed before the finishing touches could be given, and the new policy placed in harmony with the whole fiscal system.

The Budget measures of 1860 were more comprehensive even than those of 1853. The duties on food commodities that had been reduced in 1853 were now abolished, with the exception of those on cocoa, tea, and dried fruits. The differential duties on trade disappeared ; so did the last protective duties on manufactures, the 5% on woollen and 15% on silk manufactures being given up. " There will be," said Mr. Gladstone, " a sweep—summary, entire, and absolute—of what are known as manufactured goods from the face of the British tariff." The differential duties on foreign wines and brandies were removed, and provision was made for a future lower scale of rates in respect to light wines. One consequence of such extensive alterations was the attainment of a simplified customs system. Each step towards reform had struck off a good many items from the list, but the fixing of specific rates for most articles (in itself advantageous) had somewhat checked the diminution. In 1842 the number of articles chargeable was 1,052 ; by 1853 it had fallen to 466 ; in 1859 to 419. The reform of 1860 brought the number of commodities (omitting subdivisions) to 48. Even of this reduced list only fifteen were productive of revenue, five being taxed to balance duties on similar home products, and several others on account of their resemblance to the " primary " commodities. Five of the fifteen leading commodities—spirits, sugar, tea, tobacco, and wine—produced more than £1,000,000 each ; four—coffee, corn, currants, and timber—between £200,000 and £1,000,000 each ; and the remaining six—chicory, figs, hops, pepper, raisins, and rice—between £20,000 and £200,000 each. During the thirty years that have passed, the list has been further reduced : hops (1862), pepper and timber (1866), corn and rice (1869), sugar (1875), were taken out of the class of dutiable articles.

The completion of the free-trade reform was probably hastened by the negotiation of the famous French commercial treaty, the examination of which we have reserved to the present. The long protracted hostilities of the Revolutionary and Napoleonic wars had put back the commercial relations of France and England to the situation of the seventeenth century ; the tariffs of both countries were practically prohibitive of other than contraband trade. Huskisson's measures, particularly his treatment of silks and wines, were calculated to remedy this position.

Unfortunately French policy was, as we shall see, rigidly protective. A reciprocity treaty as to shipping had been concluded in 1827, but no other steps were taken to place the commerce of the two countries on a more liberal basis until Peel's second administration. Between 1842-1845, various attempts to form treaties on the reciprocal principle were tried without success. In response to the reductions of duties in England in 1842, the French duties on linens were largely increased. The effect of this policy was proved by the very trifling amount of English manufactures exported in France—£263,000 in value, besides £217,000 of machinery—in 1858.

The efforts of Cobden and Chevalier, aided by the prudence of Napoleon III and his most influential advisers, resulted in the treaty of 1860, by which terms, not indeed so favourable for England as those of 1786 but still of great service to commerce, were obtained. The reduction of the duties on wines and brandies and the abolition of protection to manufactures were part of the English stipulations ; those of France belong to the commercial policy of that country. It is noticeable that while in form the treaty was based on reciprocal concessions, England in reality surrendered nothing ; she simply continued the development of her policy on its settled course. There were, moreover, none of those conditions for exclusive advantage that marred the older treaties.

Thus at length the free-trade principle became the sole guiding rule of English commercial policy. It had taken forty years and the best endeavours of a distinguished series of statesmen to reach this point. Nothing, therefore, can be more erroneous than to regard the existing system as the product of haste or panic. If any criticism is justifiable, it is that there was undue delay in the application of recognized principles. We can hardly over-estimate the benefits that the tariff of 1860 would have been to the England of 1825. The long and bitter contest between the landed and manufacturing interests would have been avoided ; the growth of the larger English industries would have been more rapid ; the colonies would have been saved the shock that the withdrawal of their privileges after so many years undoubtedly inflicted on them ; and, most important of all, the spirit of retaliation would not have been aroused in other countries, nor could the plea have been made by foreign protectionists that it was by restriction that England became fitted for and able to endure free trade. Newmarch has shown that the delay in the Corn Law repeal from 1842 to 1845 was altogether an evil, and his statement may be extended to the whole period of reform. What was done at the end might have been done at the beginning if only the legislature had been wiser.

The time and labour expended on the English tariff enable us to understand the difficulties of commercial reforms elsewhere. Nothing but the special position of British industries and the peculiar relations of the different sections of the population made it possible to remove the favours possessed by so many producers. When continental writers object to the case of England as evidence for free trade, they may be, and are, mistaken on the question of national interest ; but they have abundant justification for the belief that the measures of our English statesmen were directly applicable only to the United Kingdom, and cannot be mechanically imitated by other countries.

In tracing the progress of reform we are in danger of forgetting the broad principles of which the various and complex enactments were the expression. The more enlightened statesmen, so early as 1820, accepted in theory the doctrine of free exchange, whatever qualifications or modifications political exigencies might compel them to allow in practice. The evidence of facts brought it home to those interested in industry that the best hope for progress lay in the opening up of fresh markets for manufactures and a reduction of the expenses of production (the *prix de revient*, as the French happily call it). Hence we have the leading canons of the commercial policy which maintained its supremacy till the outbreak of the Great European War. They are—

(1) *Complete freedom of raw materials from taxation.*—To enhance the cost of the articles used by the labour and capital of the country for further production is to handicap the industries of export and weaken industrial power,

consequently this rule was the earliest reduced to practice.

(2) *Freedom of the means of subsistence.*—Whatever difficulties may be raised as to the relation of wages to cost of production and to price, the broad fact remains that an increased price of the articles of the labourer's consumption must either raise his money wages proportionally or lower his real wages. On the former supposition the employer's gain is diminished ; on the latter the labourer's efficiency suffers. Therefore the removal of all artificial impediments to the supply of food and labourers' necessaries was an essential part of the general scheme ; the repeal of the Corn Laws was the greatest and most important instance of its application.

(3) *Abandonment of all protective differential duties on manufactures or so-called articles of luxury.*—This is perhaps the least readily intelligible part of the free-trade policy. Raw materials or food have a plain and strong claim to exemption, but special taxation of gloves, silks, wines, or of the innumerable miscellaneous manufactures may appear to only touch the rich man and to benefit the labourer. This, however, is not really so ; in the first place raw materials shade off by degrees into manufactured articles ; the finished product of one industry is the raw material of another. Again, fully manufactured articles are often essential conditions in production, as appears most plainly in respect to machinery. A modern industrial establishment requires a multiplicity of articles, and gains by getting them on the cheapest terms. Finally there is no hard-and-fast line between the " luxuries " of the rich and the consumption of the poor. The labourer's standard of comfort is not a fixed one, and the cheapening of luxuries opens their use to a wider class. As Mr. Gladstone remarked, " You may make tea or sugar or any other article of consumption the rich man's luxury if you only put on it a sufficient weight of duty." In regard to its social effects, there was no better part of the new system than its avoidance of all attempts to hinder the use of foreign manufactures.

(4) *Adoption of a simple and intelligible tariff.*—The advantage of confining duties to a moderate number of

articles is that it relieves trade from a great deal of the difficulties and restraints that attend customs supervision. There is no trouble in learning the rates of duties or in following their changes. No questions arise as to the exact duty on each particular article, the cost of collection and the pressure on commerce are diminished. Study of European tariffs will show conclusively the evils that complication produces. The absence of distinctions between colonial and foreign imports, and also of privileges to shipping, materially assist the operations of commerce. English commercial policy is still largely free trade, and for comparison with the effects of other systems of regulation it may fairly be taken as a type.

CHAPTER VII

THE ENGLISH CUSTOMS SYSTEM SINCE 1860

THE victory of free trade in the United Kingdom was for the time being complete, inasmuch as both the great political parties and the overwhelming majority of the voters supported the principle. Nor was there any need to fear a change in the active policy of the country so long as the immediate prosperity which was in part produced by the working of free trade continued to increase. But it is a perfectly well-known fact, which began to be verified at the time, that any check to trade prosperity will at once bring with it a revival, even in this country, of protectionist demands. It so happened that a series of factors coincided, especially from the beginning of the 'eighties of last century, to check somewhat the expansion of English trade and industry, and the revival of the demand for protection dates from that time.

The causes underlying the trade depression of the 'eighties can be seen much more clearly in retrospect than they were at the time. The enormous improvement in means of communication was bringing into competition with the English farmer vast areas of fertile and cheap soil. At the same time the productive capacity of Germany, France, and the United States, so far as manufacturing was concerned, was increasing, and this country experienced for the first time on a large scale the full effects of the superiority of technical education on the Continent, as compared with our own. Lastly, the demonetization of silver and the checked gold production was causing the industrial and agricultural transition to be complicated by changes in the general level of prices. Under these circumstances it was not difficult to point to evidence of temporary depression, and a Royal Commission on the

Depression of Trade found material enough for five folio volumes. One of the consequences of the depression and of the Minority Report of the Royal Commission was a revived demand for protectionist measures, taking the form in this particular case of a demand for " fair trade."

Before going into detail it is as well to notice that one other element was beginning to affect the situation. This was the rise of modern imperialism, which, as is well known, pays much attention to the value of colonial possessions and their use as potential markets. The 'eighties were the era of colonial expansion by France and Germany, and it is not surprising that this competition in " empire building " should have brought into fuller consciousness the potential resources of the British Empire. The " fair trade " movement, consequently, emphasized both the value of the colonies and what it regarded as the relative defencelessness of the United Kingdom. The Fair Trade League demanded a restriction of the time-period of commercial treaties on manufactured articles coming from countries refusing to take our manufactures duty-free, free imports of raw materials from any quarter, and, most significant of all, moderate import duties on foodstuffs from foreign countries, whilst similar imports from the British Empire were to be free, for the purpose of encouraging development of our own Empire and stimulating its growth.

We have here substantially what became known later as the demands of the " tariff reform " party. The " fair trade " agitation languished somewhat in the 'nineties, but with the turn of the century the agitation sprang into prominence, and, since 1903 at any rate, it can be said that the issue of protection or free trade remained a major one in English political life down to the outbreak of the war, the active agent in forcing the question to the front being the late Mr. Joseph Chamberlain. At this period of time it is useless to go into the motives which inspired Mr. Chamberlain at that date ; for our purposes the important point is to know the nature of his demands. He desired a strengthening of the bonds of Empire. By 1903 Canada had already granted the United Kingdom a fairly considerable preference.   The grant of colonial preferences should be interpreted as a sign that the Dominions were prepared to enter into reciprocal tariff arrangements with the United Kingdom, which would have the effect of creating a closed economic unit against the rest of the world.   It was easy to use this positive aspect of the situation as an argument for the imposition of retaliatory duties on foreign products, and thus the tariff reform agitation could represent itself as a means of binding the Empire together and also as a means of overcoming the growing hostility, or what was assumed to be the growing hostility, of foreign countries to the importation of British goods.   Whether it would have been quite so easy as the tariff reformers thought to kill two birds with one stone is a matter which we can leave on one side.   Mr. Chamberlain's practical demands took the following shape.   He desired, as the " fair traders " had done, duties on the importation of food.   There was to be a duty of 2s. a quarter on foreign corn, though maize was to be free.   There was to be a 5% duty on foreign meat and dairy produce, though here again bacon was to be free. Finally, there was to be a substantial preference on colonial wines and fruits.   These measures were advocated on the perfectly correct ground that preferences on manufactured articles would not be attractive to the colonies ; they were great food producers, and as such were primarily interested in food duties.   As compensation for these increased duties Mr. Chamberlain proposed considerable remissions of the tea and sugar duties, and corresponding reductions of the cocoa and coffee duties.   The question of whether the resulting tax scheme would have been as productive of revenue as the one which it displaced was hardly scientifically investigated by the tariff reformers at all.   As regards duties upon manufactures, Mr. Chamberlain put forward the familiar plea for the taxation of manufactured articles, suggesting an upper limit of 10%, though adhering to the free importation of raw materials, suggesting a grading of the rate of duty according to the degree of finish which the imported articles had received.

Trade improved until 1907.   In the years of depression which followed the American crisis of that year the political

situation began to be complicated by other issues, and from
1910–1913 the trade of the world leapt forward so greatly
that it was difficult to interest people in the tariff case.
The real chances of the protectionist party in this country
came with the outbreak of the Great War. It was then
found that with regard to a series of articles this country
was virtually depending on " enemy " sources of supply,
and it was now possible to link the case for protection with
the case for self-defence. From this time onwards we get
what is now the familiar demand for the protection of
" key industries." At the same time the magnificent
spirit of unity which was shown by all portions of the
Empire, and the stimulation of nationalistic feeling which
is the inevitable accompaniment of a great war, pushed
forward the question of imperial preference and stimulated
afresh the conception of an empire self-sufficing in economic
matters and confronting the world more or less as a closed
economic unit. The fact that similar schemes were being
discussed in the Central Empires gave a tremendous impetus
to the idea of a self-sufficient British Empire. In 1915 and
1916, when the Central Empires were on the whole
victorious in the field, there had been going forward a
discussion of the " Mitteleuropa scheme." It was thought
that it would be possible to organize a common customs
frontier spreading from the North Sea to the Persian Gulf.
Visions of cotton growing and wheat production in Asia
Minor, which would make the Central Empires independent
of the rest of the world as regards these two indispensable
articles, stimulated the pens of writers, and thus in the
English and the German camps alike the idea of " economic
self-sufficiency " was pushed forward. The practical
exigencies of the war further assisted the swing of opinion
towards the protectionist view. There was at once a great
demand for revenue and a considerable shortage of shipping
tonnage. The imposition of new duties, it was thought,
would at once bring in revenue and reduce the volume of
shipping space required for articles of no direct importance
in winning the war. The result was the passage in 1915
of the Finance (No. 2) Act. This Act taxed the following
articles without imposing an equivalent excise duty in the

United Kingdom : motor cars, motor bicycles, accessories and component parts of motor cars, musical instruments, accessories and component parts thereof, clocks, watches and component parts, kinematograph films.

In 1916 also there took place a Conference at Paris which, envisaging the possibility of a German victory, determined upon a common Allied commercial policy, which, had it ever been carried into effect, would have consolidated the principles of protection to a marked extent. Many of the resolutions of the Paris Conference do not concern us here, being related to the temporary exigencies of the war, but among the permanent or quasi-permanent proposals adopted at the Conference were the following :—

The refusal of most-favoured-nation treatment to many countries. The conservation of the natural resources of the Allied countries for the Allied countries before all others.

Anti-dumping measures, to take the form of prohibition of imports, and/or the inauguration of special customs *régimes* and the passing of special shipping legislation.

The prevention of enemy penetration in certain industries or professions.

Again, the Allies were to make themselves independent of enemy countries as regards raw materials and manufactured articles, essential to the normal development of economic activities, and these efforts were to cover not merely production, but also financial, commercial, and shipping organization.

There was finally to be uniform treatment of enemy patents, trade marks, and other evidences of industrial property.

While these measures represented the common policy of the Allies a further series of proposals were placed before the British public in the shape of the reports issued by the Committee presided over by Lord Balfour of Burleigh, and generally called by his name. In these reports the question of " key industries " first received full attention. Key industries were defined as those essential to national safety, as being absolutely indispensable to important British

5

industries; and, secondly, supplied entirely or mainly from enemy sources or from sources under enemy control. The general tenor of the reports of the Balfour of Burleigh Commission was in the direction of restriction, and in certain extreme cases of complete prohibition of entry.

During the war, also, the first steps were taken towards an inauguration of the policy of imperial preference. On 16 April, 1917, the Imperial War Cabinet settled upon a resolution which was afterwards (in fact on the same day), approved of by the Imperial War Conference. The terms of the resolution, so far as imperial preference was concerned, were as follow :

" The time has arrived when all possible encouragement should be given to the development of imperial resources, and especially to making the Empire independent of other countries in respect of food supplies, raw materials, and essential industries. With these objects in view this Conference expresses itself in favour of (1) the principle that each part of the Empire, having due regard to the interests of our Allies, shall give specially favourable treatment and facilities to the produce and manufactures of other parts of the Empire."

The first practical effect was the incorporation in the Finance Act of 1919 of preferences on imperial-grown or produced articles, in the case of the "breakfast-table articles," motor spirit, and tobacco, the preference being one-sixth, in the case of articles under the Finance (No. 2) Act of 1915 the preference being one-third ; and in the case of wine the preference varying from two-fifths to one-half of the normal rate of duty.

At the same time definite efforts were made during and for some time after the war to introduce a system of differential export taxes on the non-self-governing portions of the British Empire. The most celebrated of these duties was a differential duty upon palm kernels first imposed in 1916, though not in force as a matter of actual fact until 1919. In India, also, a differential export duty on raw hides and skins was introduced with a rebate of two-thirds of the duty on hides and skins exported to countries within the Empire. Thus it may be said that by the summer of

1919, when the peace treaties were signed, a considerable step had been taken towards the achievement of the principle of a self-sufficing Empire.

It now remains to trace the steps which have been taken to embody the principles of the Paris Conference and the Balfour of Burleigh Reports in practical legislation. The election policy of the Government had been dominated by the problem of reparations, notwithstanding that some attention was paid both to the question of key industries and the general issue of the protection of British capital and labour against unfair competition. In the event of a victory of the Coalition party both these groups of matters would be adhered to. Down to September, 1919, the trade policy of the Government was dominated by the now celebrated question of embargoes issued under Section 43 of the Customs Consolidation Act of 1879. The point at issue was the legality of the orders. These orders were finally challenged by a firm of chemical manufacturers whose chemicals were seized by the Customs authorities, and the constitutional problem involved was settled in the celebrated case of Rex *versus* Brown and Forth, in which action the Government lost. In November of the same year, largely as a consequence of this defeat, the first attempt was made to introduce general legislation on the subject, when the Government's first " anti-dumping " Bill—the Imports and Exports Regulation Bill—was formally introduced. The Act was so complicated and the opposition which it aroused was so great that, in spite of the notorious desire of the vast majority in the House of Commons to see such legislation passed, the Bill was never discussed in the House at all, and was not proceeded with. In fact, the first real victory of the protectionist party did not come until the end of 1920, when the Government passed the Dye-Stuffs Import Regulation Act. This Act is extremely simple in its terms. For a period of ten years the importation of dye-stuffs, colours, and colouring matters and intermediate products used in the manufacture of such dye-stuffs is prohibited. It is true that the sweeping character of these terms is mitigated by the fact that the Board of Trade was given power to issue non-transferable licences for the importation of any of the above goods. In its task of adjudicating on the requests for import licences the Board of Trade was to be assisted by a committee of five, and there was further to be an advisory committee with powers to make proposals with respect to the economical and efficient development of the dye-making industry.

The culminating point of the Government's policy was reached in 1921. In that year two Acts were passed, the Reparations Recovery Act and the Safeguarding of Industries Act. The first Act, although not strictly protectionist in intent, hampered and continues to hamper commercial intercourse between Germany and this country. It applies to all goods imported from Germany, and in general the Treasury is empowered to order that a given percentage of the value of the goods, not exceeding 50%, shall be paid by the importer to the Commissioner of Customs. The value is to be assessed on the f.o.b. value, which is stated by the Act to be the invoiced price including the sum payable to the Commissioners under the Act. The net effect of this measure has been to raise the price of German goods.

The Safeguarding of Industries Act of 1921 states in the preamble that it has been devised " with a view to the safeguarding of certain special industries and the safeguarding of employment in the United Kingdom against the effects of the depreciation of foreign currencies and the disposal of imported goods at prices below the cost of production." It is divided into two main parts, the first dealing with the safeguarding of key industries and the second dealing with the prevention of dumping. As regards key industries, a schedule to the Act enumerates the articles which shall be subject to duty under this first part, the duties in question being equal to one-third of the value of the goods. It is unnecessary here to enumerate the very large number of articles which have now been made liable to duty ; broadly speaking, the articles in question are optical glass and articles containing or implying use of optical glass, chemical glass and glassware, scientific instruments and gauges and measuring instruments, wireless valves, magnetos, arc lamp carbons, hosiery latch needles, certain compounds of rare earth metals, and all synthetic organic chemicals other than those falling under the heading of dye-stuffs. This part of the Act has already occasioned a very considerable amount of disputation and inconvenience. The fact is that interested parties may appeal to the Board of Trade either against the exclusion or inclusion of an article from lists defining the articles which are held to come under this part of the Act, and a very large number of appeals are pending before the referee appointed to settle these disputes.

Part II of the Act, which deals with dumping, defines dumping either as sale in the United Kingdom below the cost of production of the article or as sale at prices which are below those " at which similar goods can be profitably manufactured in the United Kingdom," the reason being the depreciation of the currency of the country in which the goods are manufactured. It has, however, to be shown that by reason of such dumping employment in an English industry " is being or is likely to be seriously affected." Should the Board of Trade be convinced that dumping of either of these kinds is taking place, the matter must be referred to a Committee of Inquiry. If the Committee is satisfied that complaints of dumping are justifiable, orders may be issued by which Customs duties, in addition to any duties imposed on other grounds, equal to one-third of the value of the goods may be charged upon them, though it is expressly provided by the Act that it must be proved production of the competing goods in the United Kingdom " is being carried on with reasonable efficiency and economy," and further that no such order may conflict with any " treaty, covenant, or engagement with any foreign state in force for the time being. No such order shall be valid unless and until laid before the House of Commons and approved of by resolution."

The Act, although representing a victory of the protectionist party, yet technically is much weaker than was originally intended, and this is due to the constant criticism of the free-traders in the House of Commons and outside it. The most celebrated order so far made under the Act

relates to an import duty upon fabric gloves, and this order
well illustrates the difficulties involved in any such legislation. It is agreed on all hands that the fabric gloves so
made subject to duty are manufactured in Germany from
yarn coming from English spinning mills. The imposition
of the duty therefore involves not only checking a competing product from the standpoint of British glove makers,
but also checking the exportation of a product manufactured by an important British industry.   The argument that the goods will still continue to be imported
in spite of the duty either shows the uselessness of the
legislation,   for   the   clear   object   is   to   check   such
importation as far as possible, or it shows that British
glove manufacturers are so relatively inefficient that
in spite of their rivals being handicapped by a duty of
$33\frac{1}{8}\%$ the quality of their goods is so much better that the
consumer prefers the German product.   On the other hand,
if it is asserted that the German goods will be excluded and
that compensation will be given to the Lancashire spinners
by a corresponding increase in the volume of gloves manufactured in the United Kingdom, there still remains the
question of whether the British price will be as low as the
German one, for if not, it is quite clear that demand will
fall off and a smaller quantity of yarn will be therefore
required for this purpose.   As the very object of the duty
is to prevent a cheaper product from being imported, it is
far from probable that the British price will be as low as the
German one, and consequently there is not the slightest
reason to suppose that the same volume of yarn will be
demanded for this purpose as was the case before the imposition of the duty.   A serious drafting defect in the Act was
revealed in the course of the agitation on this very matter
of fabric gloves.   The Committees of Inquiry are directed
by the Act to consider " the effect which the imposition of
a duty under this part of this Act on goods of any particular class or description would exert on employment in any
other industry, being an industry **using** goods of that class
or description as material."   The effect is that the Committees are exempted, if they take their duties in a legalist
spirit, from the task of investigating whether the imposi-

tion of a duty would hurt industries producing the raw material out of which such commodities are manufactured, and in fact the Committee which investigated the grievances of the fabric glovemakers specifically refer to the fact that the terms of the Act clearly exclude consideration of the grievances of cotton spinners. The result is only that the regular methods of procedure laid down by the Act are likely to be infringed by direct pressure on the Government and the House of Commons by any industry powerful enough to make its voice heard.

CHAPTER VIII

THE UNITED STATES TARIFF AND COMMERCIAL POLICY

THE contrast between English commercial policy and that adopted by other countries is still very decided, and nowhere is it more so than in respect to the United States. The reasons for this divergence of practical methods in the case of two countries connected by so many ties are partly historical, partly the result of differences in environment.

The natural tendencies of the American colonies, suffering as they did from the old colonial system with its many hindrances on trade, would, it might appear, have been towards complete freedom of commerce. It is quite possible that under favouring conditions this would have been the course adopted. But the very deep feeling of hostility towards England ; the belief that the industries unduly retarded by the colonial system required some compensating encouragement ; and, lastly, the pressing fiscal necessities of the new Government, combined to bring about the establishment of a moderate tariff on imported goods. The first tariff of the Federation was framed under the influence of Hamilton, who, in his famous *Report on Manufactures*, laid the basis of the later protectionism. The rates were, however, so low as to act chiefly as revenue duties, but they were increased by degrees.

More effectual than this nascent protection was the position in which the United States was placed. At first the European wars opened up a splendid market for American producers of food and raw materials, of which they largely availed themselves, as the increase in exports shows. Imports of English manufactures formed the readiest and most satisfactory mode of payment. As neutrals, the United States obtained a considerable share of the carrying trade, in spite of the English Navigation Laws. The continental system of Napoleon (1807), and the English Orders in Council (1809)—both of them gross violations of international law—stopped this rapid development. Both the imports and exports, as well as the carrying trade, fell off after 1808. Foreign markets for the flour, timber, and other materials in which a new country had special advantages were closed at first by illegal restrictions, and from 1812 by the hostile British fleet. The import of foreign manufactures suffered similarly, with the natural result that native industries sprang up, producing goods to meet the unsupplied demand. Here, as so often elsewhere, we see that war is in reality the extreme limit of protection so far as the belligerent countries are concerned.

On the conclusion of peace with England in 1814, and the European settlement of the following year, these " infant industries " were exposed to the competition of the English manufacturers, and were handicapped by the superior advantages of the " extractive " industries (i.e. those engaged in the production of food or raw materials). For their relief the tariff of 1816 imposed duties on imported goods. Cotton and woollen manufacturers were charged 25% for three years, after that date 20% ; iron about 20%, and other manufactures somewhat less. In 1815 a reciprocity treaty as to shipping was concluded with England, and was a pattern for the later treaties of Huskisson. During 1818–19 American trade passed through a time of depression, ending with a crisis in 1819. The protectionist sentiment was strengthened by this event, and after an abortive attempt at legislation in 1820, a higher tariff was passed in 1824. The duties on cotton and woollen goods were raised to $33\frac{1}{3}$%, on raw wool from 15% to 30% ; corn, lead, and hemp were also charged at higher rates, the average rate being 37%. Not satisfied with this victory, the advocates of protection pressed for further increase of duties, and by skilfully utilizing the contending political parties, they succeeded in passing the tariff of 1828, by which the duties on raw materials—wool, flax, hemp, and iron—were raised, speaking generally, to about 50%, with an additional specific duty in the case of wool.

Woollen goods were charged 40%, to increase to 50%, with *minimum* rates for the lower qualities. The duty on molasses, the basis of the rum manufacture, was doubled ; the average rate of duties was increased to 41%.

The Southern States, which were opposed to the exaggerations of the protective system, questioned the right of Congress to vote protective duties. South Carolina, under Calhoun's guidance, proposed to " nullify," or render inoperative, the tariff of 1828 ; and when this difficulty was got over, the Tariff Act of 1832 made reductions in the duties, but retained the chief protective ones with some modifications—e.g. the tax on pig-iron was lowered from $12.50 to $10 per ton ; the revenue duties were lowered, as on silk, or removed, as on tea and coffee. Notwithstanding such slight concessions, the tariff remained decidedly protective, the average rate on imported dutiable articles came to 34%. The powerful free-trade interests of the South were not satisfied, and their pressure led to the " Compromise " tariff of 1833, by which it was arranged that a gradual reduction of the high rates should take place in the next nine years, until they reached the fixed point of 20% ; the reductions, slow at first, and at intervals of two years, were to be large and rapid toward the end, and were to be completed in 1842. Thus by the process of " horizontal " reduction, as it was called, the permanent duties of the old tariff of 1816 would have been re-established. The years 1837–9 were a time of severe industrial disturbance, both in England and the United States. Numerous bank failures and a great fall in prices revived the agitation for higher duties. In 1842 a fresh measure was passed, which may be described generally as a return to the rates of 1832, though in some particular cases slightly lower ; it gave an average charge of over 30% on dutiable articles. Pig-iron paid $10, hammered-iron $17, and rolled-iron $25 per ton ; woollen goods 40%, wool three cents a pound, and 30%. This scale of duties did not remain long in force. A victory of the democratic party led to the passing of the comparatively liberal Act of 1846, prepared by Secretary Walker. The arrangement of the rates of duties was completely altered. Commodities were grouped in eight schedules, and a separate rate was fixed for the goods in each schedule. The duties varied from 100% to 5%, and on the average came to 25%. Though often described as a " free-trade " measure, it is plain that it was really one of qualified protection, not much superior to the English system before Peel's reforms. Thus iron and metal, raw or manufactured, wool and woollen goods, were in the third class and paid 30% ; cotton goods in the fourth schedule only 25%. In 1857 additional relaxation of protection was granted. Articles in the third class and cottons were henceforth only liable to 24% ; some raw materials were even admitted free of duty. The average rate fell from 25% to 20%, and remained in force till the commencement of the Civil War in 1861.

Taking the whole period from the establishment of the Constitution (1789) to the Civil War, it appears that, starting with almost nominal duties, there was a tendency shown in the tariffs of 1816–1824, and of 1828, to bring them to the point of high protection. From this point there is an opposite movement till 1842, when the protective policy takes a fresh start, which is soon checked, and the low duties continue till the close of the period. At no time was there any such system as " free trade " in the English sense. The articles on the free list varied in number, and in many cases there were no similar native productions, so that the duties were not in practice protective ; but there could be no question that considerable encouragement was always given to some important branches of manufactures, notably the cotton, woollen, and iron industries, and this aid was particularly effective in the case of the lower qualities of goods, to which the home production was mainly confined. The plan of imposing *minimum* rates of duty, in combination with a general *ad valorem* rate, had this effect—thus in 1816, the duty on cottons was 25%, but all cotton goods were to be taken as at least $25 per yard, and therefore liable to 6¼ cents duty. In 1828 the *minimum* valuation was raised to 35 cents, and soon after the price of coarse cottons was only 8½ cents, the duty being 8¾ cents or over 100%. The mixing of specific and *ad valorem* duties on a single article was another way of attaining the same object. In 1842 the duty on raw wool was placed at three cents per pound and 30% of the value, an evident favour to the coarse American wool.

The Civil War proved a decisive turning-point in fiscal policy. The revenue requirements led to an extravagant and oppressive system of taxation on both home and foreign goods. Almost every article was taxed, in many cases at every stage of its production, and to compensate native producers extra charges were put on imported goods. Just before the outbreak of the war the tariff of 1861 had established higher duties on wool and iron. The Act of 1862 raised the average rate on dutiable articles to 37%, the more extreme measure of 1864 to 47%. When, however, we remember that the concomitant internal taxation was heavy, in a few cases exceeding the import duty on the commodity, and that the cost of transport was less than formerly, these duties were not in practice as protective as the nominally lower rates of 1824 and 1828. The great industrial progress of the country acted in the opposite direction ; duties that would have been simply high revenue duties in the early part of the century, were now protective of the newer manufactures, and of the already firmly-established branches of the older ones. It is impossible to expect a careful consideration of complicated economic questions in a national crisis, when every possible mode of procuring resources has to be tried ; and therefore the high war duties had the plea of necessity for their justification.

At the close of the struggle in 1865, the position of the United States, so far as taxation and debt were concerned, had much similarity to that of England half a century before. In each case there was great complication and severity in the tax system, which fell on many commodities that affected the ordinary life of the people. Another parallel occurs after the peace. Great Britain gave up the Income Tax instead of moderating her indirect taxes. The United States commenced reductions with the internal revenue. The effect was to increase the amount of protection to the extent of the repealed internal taxes on consumption. The woollen industries, depressed after the close of the war, asked for further aid, which they obtained in 1867. Some minor changes were carried out in succeeding years. The revenue duties on tea, coffee, sugar, wine, and the protective duty on iron, were reduced in 1870 ; and in 1872 the tea and coffee duties were removed, and a general reduction of 10% of the protective duties was made ; but this percentage was replaced in 1875.

A new tariff measure, based on the report of a commission, but often departing from its proposals, was passed in 1883. Apparently intended to reduce the excessive charges on imports on the ground " that a substantial reduction of tariff duties is demanded, not by a mere indiscriminate popular clamour, but by the best conservative opinion of the country," in some directions it increased the existing rates, and left the great bulk of duties untouched. Iron received a very small reduction ; steel rails were taxed at $17 instead of $28 per ton ; the duties on wool and woollen goods in general were also reduced ; but in some of the finer classes, both of wools and cottons, there were actually increases. Linens of finer quality were lowered from 40% to 35%.

The legislation of 1883 did not succeed in settling the question of tariff reform, which increased in prominence on account of the large amount of surpluses that the existing duties brought in. Two opposite modes of meeting this difficulty were proposed, viz. (1) that of the protectionists, which would remove a sufficient number of *revenue* duties, leaving the protective ones untouched, and (2) that of the supporters of " tariff reform " who advised the placing of most raw materials on the " free list," and a proportionate reduction of the duties on manufactures. After several failures in the attempt to procure agreement between the two houses, the results of the election of 1888 enabled the former party to carry the Tariff Act of 1890 (usually known by the name of its proposer, Mr. McKinley). In its general character this measure was decidedly protectionist : though the duties on some articles were reduced, or even repealed (as e.g. in respect to raw sugar). The rates on such important classes as wool and woollen goods, metals and metal manufactures, and finally agricultural products, were seriously increased. As examples of special classes of goods treated with extreme severity, the finer linens and laces, ready-made clothing, and tin plates, may be given. The apprehensions excited in European countries as to the evil effect on several branches of trade of so rigorous a measure were soon dispelled by the remarkable revulsion of feeling in the United States in consequence of the great rise of prices that speedily followed. The election of 1892 placed the Democrats in power, and as that party was pledged to the cause of tariff reform, a somewhat conservative Tariff Bill was introduced, in December 1893, and rapidly passed through the lower House, under Mr. Wilson's guidance. In the Senate its course was less prosperous: its most important provisions for reform were reduced, and such was the effect of the Senate's hostility that, after the usual reference to a conference, the "Wilson" measure, as finally enacted (August, 1894), could hardly be regarded a breach of the protective system. Some duties were placed at even a higher point than that fixed by the Act of 1890, and a very large part of the tariff was substantially unchanged. The most important reform was the placing of wool on the free list, a privilege also conceded to flax, but not extended to iron-ore or coal, which were, however, admitted at a lower rate. The concession of free wool permitted the adoption of a simple *ad valorem* scale of duties on woollen manufactures. Slight reductions were made on silk, linen, and cotton goods ; and the heavy duty imposed by the McKinley Act on tin plates was reduced one-half ; on the other hand, raw sugar was subjected to a 4% charge. China and earthenwares may be noted as articles that received the benefit of decided reductions.

The tariff Act of 1894 was even shorter-lived than its predecessor of 1890. The Republican victory in the election of 1896, evidenced in the election of Mr. McKinley as President, was followed by the passage of the Dingley Tariff Act of 1897, which made a decided return to higher protection. Raw wool was again placed under taxation ; so were hides, which had been free from duty since 1872. Duties on manufactures were raised nearly to—in some cases higher than—the level of the Act of 1890, steel rails receiving an exceptional reduction. Specific duties were imposed on both raw and refined sugar, the latter being placed so high as to give protection to the manufacturers. The Dingley tariff of 1897 was not altered for twelve years. The impulse to revision came from a gradually rising wave of public sentiment against what was considered to be the domination of American industrial and social life by the enormous aggregations of capital which were, and are, somewhat inaccurately known as trusts. The intellectual basis of the revision of 1909 was that of " equalizing the cost of production." As Professor Taussig has pointed out, this argument, taken logically, admits of very high protection if one selects extreme cases ; for, logically, if it is considered desirable to equalize the cost of production in all cases, the least efficient industry would require enormously high protection to enable it to conduct its operations. The Payne-Aldrich tariff of 1909 contained certain reductions, and would have contained more had it not been for the opposition of interested parties, which was only in part overcome by the stand taken by President Taft, who sincerely believed in the necessity for moderation in the degree of tariff protection granted. Some of the reductions, e.g. on iron and steel goods, were useless since the growth of an enormous iron and steel industry had virtually given the home manufacturers a complete control over their own market. Hides were freed, but the original proposals for the free importation of coal, iron, and lumber were not carried. Consequential on the freeing of hides came a reduction in the duties on leather goods. It is significant that the attempt to cause a reduction of the Canadian export duties on certain types of timber required for pulp were not successful, in spite of the inclusion in the tariff of specially-devised retaliatory duties.

If the tariff contained reductions it also imposed increased duties in important respects. Thus there were increases in the textile schedules, especially on cotton goods and on silk. The wool schedules were substantially unchanged by the new tariff. The reduction of five cents on refined sugar was practically ineffective.

The 1909 tariff provided for the imposition of a maximum as well as a minimum rate of duty. The rates actually embodied in the tariff were to be regarded as the minimum rates, and provision was made for an increase of 25% in the duty leviable in those cases in which foreign countries discriminated against the products of the United States. In fact, however, this provision was never put into force. The discretion vested in the President remained practically ineffective.

Between 1909–1913 the wave of reaction against the domination of American economic life by powerful industrial and financial corporations increased. At the same time circumstances came to the aid of the opponents of high protection. A rise in the cost of living occurred practically simultaneously all over the world, and this was naturally made use of by the Democratic Party and reinforced the case for reduction. The Democrats found in President Wilson a powerful and eloquent leader, and the fact that a Democratic President was supported in both Houses of Congress by a Democratic majority enabled the Democratic Party to revise the tariff and to pass in 1913 a tariff which is generally known as the Underwood tariff. Again it was found necessary to devise a theoretical formula to justify the action actually taken. The Democrats urged the necessity for a competitive tariff. This again is by no means a very clear formulation of what is desirable, but the practical application referred to what were considered to be the very often excessive profits which were being made under the shelter of the 1909 protective rates. But, as Professor Taussig also points out, the demand for a competitive tariff leaves the road open in doubtful cases for an upward as well as a downward revision of rates.

However that may be, the general tendency of the Underwood tariff was to revise rates in a downward direction, though in many cases the reductions were purely nominal. The reductions served, says Professor Taussig, " to lower duties that had been prohibitory or to abolish duties that had been nominal. Much the larger part of the changes were probably of this sort."

The import of raw wool was freed at once. As a consequence the specific compensatory duties on woollen goods were also abolished. The *ad valorem* duties on woollen goods were reduced from a level of 50–55% to a general level of 35%. In the case of cotton goods only *ad valorem* duties were now imposed. On cotton cloths the duties varied between 5% and 30% ; on hosiery between 20% and 40% ; on knit goods they were 30%, and on gloves they were 35%. In the case of silk the duties remained relatively high. Here also *ad valorem* duties were substituted for specific duties, the rates of duty being 45% to 50% on velvets and plushes. In the case of iron and steel goods some raw materials were freed, e.g. iron ore, pig iron, scrap, steel rails, and barbed wire. On the remaining articles the duties ran from 5% to 20% ; but, as already pointed out, the American iron and steel industry so completely dominated the home market that these reductions were only nominal.

Agricultural machinery was freed, boots and shoes were added to the free list, and so were a number of important articles of food-stuffs—wheat, cattle, flour, meat, eggs, and milk. The sugar duty was to disappear after 1916 and was reduced for the time being. Coal and lumber, the duties on which had been reduced in 1909, were also added to the free list.

At the same time important changes were made in the administrative provisions of the tariff, which we cannot go into here. The double tariff provision of 1909 disappeared and the tariff again became a single rate tariff.

American opinion is on the whole so decidedly protectionistic in tone that tariff reductions are generally short-lived. The Underwood tariff was followed by the European War, and from 1917 onwards by the participation of the United States in that conflict. It was therefore almost inevitable that the heightened nationalistic sentiment, which reached levels in America which left those of Europe far behind, should react on the policy with regard to tariff rates. The resentment which was felt in America whilst it was still neutral at certain incidents of the blockade policy of the United Kingdom had already led to a revision of certain aspects of the tariff in 1916 ; Section 801 of the United States Revenue Act of that year had introduced the conception of " unfair competition," which was declared to

6

be an unlawful act. But the conclusion of the European conflict brought much more startling changes with it. In 1918 resentment at the war policy of the Wilson administration had given the Republicans a majority in Congress. Business men in all the Allied countries were filled with fear as to the possible competitive ability of the Central European Powers, and this reinforced the fear, always latent in the American mind, of the competition in American markets of the pauper labour of Europe. But it was overlooked by the Republican Party that the position of America had altered considerably as a consequence of the war. Before the war America had been the great debtor nation of the world. Her railways were very largely European-owned, and a constant stream of goods was sent across the Atlantic in payment of interest on European-owned securities. The post-war situation was exactly the opposite. The pre-war investments of Europe had very largely been resold, and an enormous debt had been contracted by European states in the United States, interest upon which had now to be paid. The phenomenon of America as lender rather than borrower did not cease with the Armistice. Heavy commitments were entered into by private individuals and governments after actual fighting had ceased. Moreover, America had become a great ship-owning nation. If profitable employment were to be found for American shipping it was clearly in the interest of American shipowners to stimulate the movement of goods in both directions, for an inadequate compensation of outward-moving cargo by inward-moving cargo implies an uneconomical working of shipping.

Adherence to a high tariff policy under these circumstances obviously is a much more serious matter than it was before the war. The growing desire of the American financial and banking world, if not to usurp the position of London, at any rate to become coeval with it, was likely to be imperilled by a policy which hampered the debtors (public and private) of the United States in paying their debts, and was clearly inconsistent with the maintenance of New York as a great financial centre. The opposition of the financial interests had therefore to be overcome, the

Republicans abandoning their traditional alliance with the moneyed interest and falling back upon the American farmer. Suspicion of Wall Street and the trading interests are powerful factors in the American agricultural situation, where for some time past a desperate battle has been fought for the freeing of the American farmer from the supposed clutches of the money power.[1] The position of the consumer, suffering from high prices, the effect in the main of inflation, might, it would have been thought, have acted as a barrier to a protectionist revival. The consumer's antipathy to adding burdens to those he was already shouldering was overcome owing to the fact that the tariff was not a leading feature in the election which gave the Republicans their power, and in any case a high tariff fits in well with the nationalistic sentiments which did in fact throw the Democrats out of office. There have been two tariff Acts since the Armistice. The first was an emergency Act passed in May, 1921 ; the second the Fordney Act, which received presidential approval in September, 1922. The importance of the emergency tariff lies mainly in the fact that it granted protection on agricultural produce and strengthened considerably the law relating to anti-dumping duties. Among the agricultural duties imposed were a duty of 35 cents per bushel on wheat, a 30% duty on cattle, a duty of 2 cents per ton on fresh or frozen meat, duties on butter and butter substitutes, cheese and milk, fruits, rice, maize, peas, potatoes, and edible oils.

At the same time duties were imposed on raw cotton (7 cents per pound), together with an equivalent compensating duty on manufactured cotton goods, and duties on wool, the rates being 15 cents on unwashed wool, 30 cents on washed wool, and scoured wool 45 cents. Again, compensating duties were added to manufactured wools.

The Fordney tariff deals not only with agricultural duties, but revises the whole tariff. It is described by Professor H. Parker Willis as " Unquestionably . . . both actually and potentially the highest general Tariff Law

[1] But the main direct factor was the fall in the prices of agricultural products.

ever enacted in the history of Protection. It can be described in moderate terms as Protectionism carried almost to the height of insanity, and may easily result in practically suspending the importation of goods, with the exception, of course, of absolutely essential manufacturers' materials, and with the further exception, probably, of such articles of luxury as appeal to a purchasing public which is largely indifferent to price."

In estimating the burden imposed on trade by the tariff of 1922 one has to distinguish between the direct effect of the rates embodied in the various schedules and the effects of the administrative provisions which are also contained in the tariff. The burden of a duty in so far as it is assessed on values varies with the value ascertained. When the Act passed the House of Representatives it embodied what was known as the " American valuation system " ; that is to say, the duties were to be assessed not on the real value of the goods—" foreign valuation "—but upon the value of competing American goods. The phrase " a competitive tariff " really sums up the underlying idea which is still embodied in the tariff as it left the Senate ; for although the general principle of American valuation has been rejected, nevertheless in certain not impossible cases the American valuation can be adopted, and the clauses of Title 3, in which the special provisions are embodied, frequently refer to " differences in conditions of competition." A further element of importance in assessing the burden of the tariff is the discretionary power invested in the American President, which will enable him under certain circumstances not only to change the basis of valuation, but also to increase the substantive rate of duty, whether specific or *ad valorem*. Further, a series of provisions enable the President to raise duties in cases of unfair competition and in cases of discrimination against the products of the United States by foreign countries ; and " discrimination " against the United States applies not only to actual charges imposed but also to indirect discrimination " by law or administrative regulation or practice, by or in respect to any duty, fee, charge, exaction, classification, regulation, condition, restriction, or prohibition, in such manner as to place the commerce of the United States at a disadvantage compared with the commerce of any foreign country." The President has further the power to take action when a foreign product is bounty-fed. In cases of unfair competition and discrimination the retaliatory measures which can be taken by the President go so far as to permit the total exclusion of the articles concerned from the United States altogether. The President is empowered to raise duties by not more than 50% of the rate specified in the Act in cases in which the existing duties do not equalize differences in costs of competition, or in cases in which articles wholly or in part the growth or product of the United States are materially injured by foreign imports. In this latter case the President is further empowered to change the basis of valuation.

Generally the value of imported merchandise is taken to be the foreign value or export value, whichever is higher. If either of these values cannot be ascertained, then the United States value is substituted. If there is neither a foreign value, an export value, nor a United States value, then the cost of production is substituted. The Act further gives power to inspect the books of exporters to the United States and similar documents relating to importers. In the event of refusal, the importation of merchandise on account of such exporter or importer may be prohibited, and delivery of merchandise by or to such persons may also be stopped. At the end of one year, if the importer or exporter still continues to refuse inspection, such goods may be sold at public auction. Retaliatory provisions are not entirely excluded even from the rate schedules themselves. Thus a Paragraph 1,610 in the free list schedule only permits the importation of mechanically-ground wood pulp free of duty, subject to the absence of export duties or other restrictions in the country of export, otherwise a 10% *ad valorem* duty, and in addition an amount equal to such export duty, is leviable ; and the same general provisions apply to standard news-print paper under Section 1,659. In the case of wood in Paragraph 1,683 freedom of importation is contingent on the absence of import duties upon similar products from the United States. If after negotiations import duties upon American products are not removed, the United States shall impose duties equal in amount on the products from the area in question. The rate schedules of the Act are divided into 1,690 paragraphs, but the number of separate rates is very much greater than this, since many of the paragraphs cover a very large number of separate articles and separate rates.

The preceding review of the stages of more than a century of tariff legislation brings out the principles that have been gradually developed in the United States as to commercial policy. The contrast they present to the British system, described in the preceding chapter, is truly remarkable, as will be even more readily perceived by stating them in the form of propositions, which will run as follow : —

(1) Native industries are entitled to reasonable protection against foreign competition. (2) A customs tariff is the most convenient mode of raising revenue, and preferable to internal taxation. (3) Unmanufactured articles of general consumption—tea, coffee, sugar, etc.—should be either admitted free or very lightly taxed. (4) Raw materials may fairly be taxed, the native manufacturer who works them up being compensated by an additional import duty on his product. (5) Imported manufactured articles are peculiarly fit subjects for high taxation, since the foreign producer suffers by the duties which help to encourage home industry. (6) The scale of duties has to be determined, not simply with reference to the revenue required but, too, with consideration of the protection needed by the several industries. (7) As a consequence, the tariff can be neither uniform nor simple ; it must include numerous articles, yielding little or no revenue, and it must attempt to discriminate between commodities that closely resemble each other.

Each of these principles may be illustrated from any of the United States tariffs, from the so-called free-trade one of 1857, as well as from the protectionist ones of 1828, 1864, 1890, 1897, 1909, and 1922. The least authoritatively established is the fourth. It seemed at times as if raw materials would escape duties ; but wool, after a brief exemption, has been replaced on the list of dutiable imports, and its example has helped to keep other objects in the same position. The presentation of definite principles, as exemplified in tariff legislation, is in one way misleading. It suggests that the system of duties is the result of careful and well-planned arrangement. To say that it is always the outcome of compromise would be nearer the truth. Every tariff Act has turned on the struggles of sectional or industrial interests ; the South against New England and the West in the earlier periods ; after the war the claims of the various large industries. The final result is a mixture of conflicting aims that seriously detracts from the effective working of the measure. Writers of opposite opinions on the question of the best commercial policy are agreed on the existence of this evil. " The history of tariff-making," says Mr. Bolles, " is not particularly honourable in all its details to any party or interest ; it has too often partaken of a personal fight by manufacturers against the public and each other." This feature of American tariffs is so obvious that it deserves to be stated as a part of their history rather than as a criticism.

CHAPTER IX

THE REFORM OF CONTINENTAL TARIFFS, 1815–1865

THE French Revolution, and the movements that followed it, effectually broke up the old European system. This transformation was not confined to political conditions. Economic life came under new influences. The old method of government, and the " liberalism " that assailed it, had both to be modified in order to fit them for the changed position of society.

The long continuance of war had in some cases checked commerce, and in more driven it into indirect channels. Exports and imports were both open to the high-handed interference of the French and the very strict regulations of the English. Many industries in continental countries attributed their existence to the advantages that the continental system had given them, and now that peace was restored, claimed the aid of the state against foreign competition. The sudden influx of English manufactures was regarded as a serious danger, only too likely to happen unless sufficient precautions were taken against it. The course pursued by European statesmen for the period 1815–1860 is only explicable by bearing this circumstance fully in mind. The development of the different tariffs shows how it operated.

To begin with the country that would appear peculiarly fitted for the closest trade relations with Great Britain—France—we find that at the close of the war in 1814, the duties then levied (fixed in 1806) favoured the woollen and cotton industries ; in other respects they followed those of 1791, already mentioned (p. 42). Commerce with England was prohibited by the war, and dealing in English goods was a violation of the decrees of Napoleon ; but an extensive contraband trade existed, and licences were freely given which permitted traffic in the otherwise forbidden commodities. At the Restoration some slight modifications were made, but they were only temporary. The protectionist spirit was strong in the Royalist party, as the Corn Laws of 1819 and 1821 (which established a complicated sliding scale on the English model), and the tariff of 1822, showed. The industrial and commercial depression, then so general, contributed to bring about the increase of the duties on foreign sugar, cattle, flax, wool, and many smaller articles. In 1826 an aggravation of the protective duties was carried, the charge on wool being raised to 30%, that on steel to 100%.

The Orleanist Government succeeded in getting a moderate reduction of some of the most oppressive duties, but was unable or unwilling to change the main parts of the system, which remained rigidly protective, the import of certain important goods being altogether prohibited. Between 1840–1850 there were even some increases of protection due to the pressure of the interested producers.

The first serious attempt to alter this very severe restrictive system was reserved for the Second Empire. The English reforms of Peel proved the possibility of removing most of the barriers to commerce that legislation had set up, and consequently Napoleon III entered with moderation on the work of revision. Between 1853 and 1855 the duties on coal, iron, steel, and wool were lowered, as also those on cattle, corn, and various raw materials, the requirements for shipbuilding being allowed in free. The legislative body was, however, with difficulty brought to consent to these measures. A more extensive proposal— made in 1856—to remove all prohibitions on imports, while retaining protective duties of 30% on woollen and 35% on cotton goods, had to be withdrawn, in consequence of the strong opposition that it excited. The interest of the consumers was in the popular opinion entirely subordinate to that of the iron-masters, cotton-spinners, and agriculturists—one of the many instances which shows that the long continuance of high duties does not facilitate the introduction of free competition.

It was under such discouraging circumstances that the famous Commercial Treaty of 1860 with England was negotiated. This important measure (the work of Chevalier and Cobden, but owing a good deal of its success to the efforts of the Emperor and M. Rouher), though only a finishing step in English tariff reform (p. 57), inaugurated a new era in France. All prohibitions of imports disappeared, and were replaced by protective duties not to exceed 30% (this maximum ultimately to descend to 25%). The rates, first determined by the value, were to be converted into specific duties by a later convention. The working out of these details was managed by Cobden, whose vivid account of the troubles of his task recalls to mind the similar difficulties that impeded the application of the treaty of 1786. It is, however, curious to notice that in several points the later treaty was less liberal. Nevertheless it placed the commercial intercourse of France and England on a new footing, and led to a rapid growth of trade between them.

A further advantage was the initiation of a policy, that was so largely followed by other countries that the European states were gradually bound together by a network of treaties, securing a lower scale of duties. The operation of the "most-favoured-nation" clause, as it is called, by which the contracting parties bind themselves to give each other whatever privileges may be given to any third power), was most effective in this respect. A reduction of duties, granted by one state in respect to the goods imported from another, was applicable equally to all countries having treaties. Accordingly the "conventional" or treaty tariff became quite distinct from the general tariff, which was only effective when there was no treaty—an exceptional case.

The reforms of the French Government were not confined to those accomplished by treaty regulations. The same sentiments that brought about the concessions to foreign countries of a more moderate scale of charges on their goods led to amendments by direct legislation. Some of the worst parts of the protectionist system were removed. The Corn Laws, with their complex sliding scale and division of the country into different regions according to the supposed cost of producing wheat, had been so inconvenient in practice that they were frequently suspended ; but in 1861 the bolder step of complete repeal was taken, and a nominal fixed duty of 60 centimes per 100 kilos (3d. per cwt.) was imposed instead. The duty on cattle was similarly treated, an imperial decree to that effect being confirmed by legislation in 1863.

The broad general effect of these measures was the transformation of the very severe system that the Restoration had established into one of low duties and moderate protection on manufacturers. The economic result was a large increase of both imports and exports, the former of which rose from 1,641 million francs (£65,600,000) in 1859 to 3,153 million francs (£126,000,000) in 1869, while the latter grew from 2,266 million francs (£90,600,000) in 1859 to 3,075 million francs (£123,000,000) in 1869—that is, a total increase in ten years nearly approaching £100,000,000. Manufacturing industries were special gainers, owing to the reductions or abolitions of duty on the most important raw materials.

The commercial policy of France would naturally have a powerful effect on the smaller neighbouring states, but we find that some of them had preceded her in the commencement of reform. Thus, though Sardinia up to 1849 was strongly protectionist, the influence of Cavour altered this attitude, and a series of measures in 1851, 1852, and 1853 softened the rigour of the previous regulations. Agricultural products and various raw materials were subjected to moderate charges, or allowed to enter in freedom. The expansion of Sardinia into the kingdom of Italy enabled the same policy to be applied to the whole country, most of which had been previously regulated as to duties by Austria.

Holland, which had been under the protective *régime* till 1847, in that year followed England in repealing its corn laws. It abandoned its special duties on foreign shipping in 1850, and carried out a general tariff reform in 1854. Belgium at the same time made similar progress in the direction of freedom, giving up corn laws and reducing differential duties in 1850 and 1852 ; in 1856 the differential duties were removed, and in the following year raw materials were admitted free. Switzerland had no general tariff until

1849, when as a result of the constitution of the preceding year a uniform scale of duties was arranged, but without protection. Portugal had carried out several reforms in 1852, and even Spain in some degree departed from the prohibitive duties that were imposed previous to 1849.

The effect of the Anglo-French commercial treaty was to stimulate further action in the same course. Treaties were concluded by Belgium with France (1861) and England (1862), a course followed by Italy in 1863. Spain was slower in adopting a liberal policy, and her relations with England were specially affected by the higher rates charged in this country on the strong Spanish wines. The first step towards reform was made by Figuerola's administration in 1868.

The situation of Germany, or rather the German States, was in such sharp contrast to that of France that the development of commercial policy almost necessarily differed widely. The turning-point in German commercial policy was the formation of the *Zollverein*, or customs union, which was the first step towards national unity. This league commenced with the smaller unions of Prussia, and Hesse Darmstadt (1832), Bavaria, and Wurtemberg (1828), and Hanover, Brunswick, and Oldenburg (1834). By 1833 the central portion comprised a population of over 25,000,000, and the most important states of the Germanic Confederation (Austria excepted). Its original scale of duties was based on the moderate Prussian tariff of 1818, which made import duties the chief source of the customs revenue, export dues being lowered. By it protection to manufacturers was limited to 10%, besides a uniform duty of 1s. 6d. per cwt. on all goods, and therefore heaviest on cheap and bulky articles. Within the customs union protectionist sentiments soon became noticeable. The adoption of a national policy was advocated by a section having List, the founder of so-called scientific protectionism, for its leader, but the necessity for unanimity among the states in order to carry any change tended to preserve the old duties. In 1842 certain alterations in the direction of higher protection were made, the duties on cotton yarns were raised, and pig-iron, previously free, was

subjected to 20s. per ton. The maintenance of the English
Corn Laws encouraged this movement as a form of retaliation on England for her exclusion of the raw materials
produced in Germany.

The course of events after 1850 tended to weaken the
protectionist feeling ; and in 1853 numerous reductions were
carried out in connexion with a commercial treaty with
Austria, by which the whole German territory of the time
received the advantage of comparative freedom of
commerce.

The tendency towards free trade was strengthened by the
Anglo-French treaty, which enabled the advocates of a
liberal commercial policy to secure the adoption of a like
engagement between France and Prussia (1862), finally
extended so as to include the whole *Zollverein* (1865).
In the latter year a treaty was also negotiated with England.
As a result, the whole tariff of the league was reformed.
The general import duty of 1s. 6d. per cwt. was removed ;
so were the duties on corn and other agricultural products ;
on wood, and on many manufactures and chemicals. In
fact, the new tariff was a large instalment of free trade.

Up to 1851 the Austrian tariff, regulated by the measures
of 1822 and 1838, had been of a restrictive character ; but
the general current of liberal sentiment then led to the
above-mentioned treaty with the German *Zollverein*, and
though the engagement lapsed in 1862, the existing policy
of low duties was continued.

The Russian Empire had been long notorious for the
extremes to which the protectionist system had been
carried. A slight reduction of duties in 1821 was followed
by a sharp rise in 1823, which was maintained by the advice
of the finance minister Count Cancrin, whose writings
evidence the connexion between the old mercantile system
and the newer protectionism. In 1851 and 1855 some concessions were made to the necessities of foreign trade ; however, no serious inroad on the existing barriers was
attempted.

In the foregoing brief outline of European tariff history
it is easy to see the working of general forces. Protection—
in many cases prohibition—was the rule for the first part

of the period, Prussia and Switzerland being the only noticeable exceptions. About 1850 a more liberal influence is perceptible. Reductions of duties become, so to speak, fashionable. Every country is examining its regulations and seeking to revise them. The French treaty is a kind of landmark, as being the adoption of a new method of reform, and its extension places the tariff systems of Europe, in a great degree, on a new basis. As a result, four general principles of commercial policy are for the time recognized in (1) the abandonment of prohibitions, (2) the almost complete relief of raw materials from duty, (3) the fixing of moderate duties on imported manufactures, and (4) the surrender of discrimination against particular countries. Though the result was not (as is often imagined) the attainment of pure free trade, it was of the utmost importance for European progress. The growth of commerce and the development of industry were not indeed due to this or to any single case. A number of agencies were together in operation—the expansion of the railway system and of steam navigation, the new supplies of gold, and the more liberal commercial policy. Each contributed its share to the final result, and it is difficult to assign the separate proportions ; but there is little rashness in conjecturing that the part of the last-named was not the smallest. Improved means of transport are of little use if they are off-set by artificial hindrances, while the stimulus of increased stocks of the precious metals is at best temporary. The opening up of a wider area of international trade has a permanent effect proportional to the extent of the new field added.

To realize more fully the rapidity of the formation of new treaties, we may take the particular case of France. Between 1860 and 1867 she concluded fourteen treaties, viz., with England (1860), Belgium (1861), Prussia and the *Zollverein* (1862), Italy (1863), Switzerland (1864), Sweden and Norway, the Hanse towns, Mecklenburg, and Spain, (1865), Holland, Portugal, Austria, and Japan (1866) the States of the Church (1867). When we remember that each of the other nations had an equally long list, we can understand the effect produced.

The growth of liberal sentiments was evidenced not only

by reductions of import duties, but by relaxations of other forms of restriction. Greater facilities for the transit trade (or movement of foreign goods through a country) were granted, as well as for the storage of imports for ultimate re-export. The old Navigation Laws were, as we have noticed, entirely repealed or greatly modified, and such colonial trade as the continental states possessed was placed on a more liberal footing. The bounty system was curtailed with great financial benefit.

In fine, we may say that partly by treaty agreements, but also in part by independent national legislation, the protective system was changed, not with the same vigour or thorough consistency as marked English policy, but still, considering the difficulties that popular sentiment placed in the way, with considerable judgment and very decided advantage to the economic interest of the countries concerned.

Another feature of the political development of Europe that assisted the advance of commerce was the widening of the areas to which the customs systems applied. We have seen one notable instance in the German customs union ; another was the establishment of Italian unity.

A less obvious consequence of these changes was that while freedom of intercourse was increased, foreign commerce in the narrow sense was in some respects less necessary. In the present state of industry, a small territory is compelled to draw its supplies of many articles from outside. A large and populous nation is not. France, Germany, or Russia could at need obtain most of what is absolutely requisite for their wants from their own areas. All the leading industries of modern life are represented in each of these states, and the natural desire of producers to control the home market obtains a plausible basis in the capacity that they possess of meeting the national demand for their products. This, among other circumstances, has aided the reactionary movement that is a characteristic of the present time.

The reforms, political and economic, of the half century from 1815 have thus in part supplied the material for a partial reversal of the policy on which they were founded.

CHAPTER X

EUROPEAN TARIFFS (1865–1920).—THE
PROTECTIONIST REACTION

THE more ardent free traders believed that the adoption
of their system by England, and the large portion of it
extended to other countries by the treaties described in
the last chapter, marked a definite step in the progress of
economic policy. Protectionist ideas were thought to be
obsolete and fated to disappear before the diffusion of sound
ideas on the nature of commerce. The course of events
during the last fifty years has given a rude shock to these
sanguine anticipations. Far from winning new ground,
the upholders of commercial freedom were compelled to
fight for what had been previously gained, and a survey of
existing tariffs shows a general rise of duties over those of
the period of liberal ascendancy.

The causes of this change are various and differ in different countries, but some stand out so prominently that
there is little trouble in detecting them. First of all the
wars that have been a conspicuous feature of the period
tended to limit the former liberal policy. National sentiment is aroused by warfare, but unless enlightened beyond
the existing standard of popular knowledge on economic
matters, it desires to encourage, as it thinks, native industries by excluding the products of the foreigner, who is or
may be an enemy. Warfare is, besides, under modern
conditions extremely costly, and high customs duties, with
accompanying protection, are the easiest way of gaining the
requisite supplies. The exigencies of finance give support
to the sentiment of protection. How important this
influence is will appear from later details ; it is, generally
speaking, true that the need of fresh revenue is a condition
precedent to an increase of protection. Another and more

special cause has also worked in the same direction.   At no former period has the development of the resources of new countries been carried on with equal vigour and success. New fields of supply for the markets of Europe have been opened up, with the necessary result of reducing the cost of agricultural products much below the former level.   The advantage to consumers is undeniable, but the immediate loss to producers is also great.   In particular the classes interested in agriculture have suffered from a depreciation of their land and capital that has placed them in serious difficulties.   The widespread economic dislocation which was the result of cheaper sources of supply, supplemented by improved means of transport, has, along with many benefits, brought some disadvantages.   In a large modern nation it is hopeless to expect that production will be all at once adjusted to economic changes, but without rapid adjustment some loss is inevitable.   Thus the agricultural depression, very general in Europe, led to a strong feeling in favour of meeting the evil by removing its proximate cause, which is believed to be the importation of foreign " food-stuffs."

What facilities of transport and extended cultivation have done for agriculture, the progress of mechanical invention and of business organization has done for manu-factures.   The methods of production and the system of conducting business are both worked at a higher speed and subjected to much more severe competition from abroad ; the old practical monopolies possessed by special localities or countries have become merely advantages that are pre-carious and retained only by care and energy.   Countries in which neither agriculture nor manufactures are highly developed are therefore exposed to a double pressure ; they cannot compete with success in foreign markets, and in their own a fall of prices is necessary to enable their com-paratively superior industries to hold their ground.   In such a case the imposition of duties to protect industries all round is the most obvious way (to the popular mind) of meeting the evil, and until its real effects are impartially examined, it possesses a certain plausibility.

As movement in a given direction continues after the

7

original impetus is withdrawn, so we shall see that in some instances the progress of reform was persisted in to a recent time, and that the decided protectionist reaction dates only from about 1877, though of course it was earlier in some countries than in others.

The Franco-German War (1870–1) and the overthrow of Napoleon III at once arrested the free-trade policy, which had little support in the national mind, and was hardly understood outside the small circle of French economists. The need of fresh revenue was imperative, and M. Thiers, the most prominent of French statesmen, was notoriously protectionist in his leanings. Pure revenue duties on colonial and Eastern commodities were first tried ; the sugar duty was increased 30% ; that on coffee was trebled ; tea, cocoa, wines, and spirits, were all subjected to greatly increased charges. As the yield thus obtained did not suffice, proposals for the taxation of raw materials were brought forward but rejected by the legislature in 1871, when M. Thiers tendered his resignation. To avoid this result the measure was passed, not however to come into operation until compensating protective duties had been placed on imported manufactures.

The existing commercial treaties were a further obstacle to changes in policy, and accordingly negotiations were opened with England and Belgium, in order that the new duties might be applied to their products. As was justifiable under the circumstances, the former country required that if imported raw products were to be taxed, the like articles produced in France should pay an equivalent tax, and therefore, as the shortest way of escape, the French Government gave notice for the termination of the treaties (in the technical language of international law "denounced" them), and new conventions were agreed on ; but as this arrangement was just as unsatisfactory in the opinion of the French Chambers, the old treaties were in 1873 restored to force until 1877, and thus the larger part of the raw materials escaped the new taxation.

The protectionist tendency was, too, manifested in the departure from the open system introduced in 1866 in respect to shipping. A law of 1872 imposed differential duties on goods imported in foreign vessels, with a charge of three francs per 100 kilos (1s. 3d. per cwt.) on goods in store for export, besides a so-called quay duty. A plan for a series of export duties failed to pass, but a statistical duty of 1d. on each package, ton of goods in bulk, or head of animals, either imported or exported, was carried, with the ostensible object of defraying the official expenses. The advance of the sentiment in favour of a return to the restrictive system was even more decidedly indicated in 1881. Bounties were then granted for the encouragement of French shipping, and extra taxes imposed on indirect imports of non-European and some European goods. In 1889 the carrying trade between France and Algiers was reserved for native ships.

The revision of the general tariff was a more serious task, undertaken with a view to influencing the fresh treaties that the termination of the old engagements made necessary. The tariff of 1881 (to come into force in 1882) made several increases and substituted many specific for *ad valorem* duties. Raw materials escaped taxation; half-manufactured articles were placed under moderate duties. The nominal corn duties were diminished by a fraction, but the duties on live stock and fresh meat were considerably increased, oxen from 3s. to 12s. per head, sheep from 3d. to 1s. 8d., and other animals in proportion ; fresh meat from 3d. to 1s. 3d. per cwt., while salt meat was slightly reduced.

A new " conventional " tariff speedily followed in a series of fresh treaties with European countries. Agreements with Belgium, Italy, Portugal, Sweden, and Norway were concluded in 1881, with Spain and Switzerland in 1882, and with Serbia in 1883. The Austro-French treaty of 1879 was continued, and a convention for " most-favoured-nation " treatment on each side was signed by England and France in 1882. Germany continued to receive the same privilege by the treaty of 1871.

The duties on whole or partially-manufactured goods remained substantially unchanged by the new treaties, which did not, in fact, vary so much from the general tariff as was previously the case. The number of articles included in the conventions had been reduced, and all countries outside Europe came under the general code. The reaction against the liberal policy of 1860 was thus as yet very slight, and did not seriously affect manufactures.

The agricultural depression was the primary cause of the legislation of 1885, which placed a duty of 3 francs per quintal on wheat, 7 francs on flour, 2 francs on rye and barley, and 1 franc on oats, with additional duties on indirect importation. Cattle, sheep, and pigs came under increases of 50% to 100%—e.g. the tax on oxen was raised to £1 per head ; that on pigs from 2s. 6d. to 5s. ; sheep to 2s. 6d. As this measure did not bring about the expected relief, most of the duties were raised still higher in 1887— wheat to 5 francs, oxen to 30s. per head, sheep to 4s. ; fresh meat to 12 francs for 100 kilos.

A more decided step towards protection was made by the measure of 1892, under which two scales of tariff were arranged, the lower one to apply to those countries only that should conclude commercial treaties with France.

The tariff thus became a double autonomous one, for France was left free, in spite of the conclusion of treaties, to alter not only the general rates, but also the minimum rates ; so that, although there was a temptation to enter into commercial agreements with France, nevertheless her freedom of action was much greater than it would have been had she concluded customs treaties of the ordinary type, in which her ability to manipulate the conventional rates would have been limited for the lifetime of the treaty. The inauguration of a new tariff *régime* was not without its difficulties. A tariff war with Switzerland ensued, which lasted from 1893 to July, 1895, and resulted on the whole in a victory for the Swiss.

The French tariff of 1892 remained substantially unaltered till 1910. New industries had in the meantime sprung up and it was also believed that the difference between the maximum and minimum duties in the 1892 tariff was not enough to make the application of a maximum rate sufficiently awe-inspiring. The tariff of 1910 was largely the work of the two Chambers ; the Government on the whole exercised a moderating influence. The tariff was marked by an increase of the difference between the maximum and minimum schedules, at the same time that the whole height of the tariff wall was raised, attention being largely concentrated on the metal schedules.

There has been no general tariff revision in France since the end of the war, but such a revision cannot be delayed very much longer.   France has now become, in virtue of the reacquisition of Alsace and Lorraine, one of the largest iron producing countries of the world.   In addition, the very important Alsace cotton industry is now within the French tariff frontier.   These two facts are bound to influence the future of French tariff policy.   What has been done since the war has been to apply a system of " co-efficients " to the existing tariff, by means of which it has become possible to adapt the overwhelmingly specific nature of the tariff to the rise in prices which occurred since the war.   Since the Government is perfectly free to vary these coefficients as it likes by governmental decree, it has acquired a power over the tariff wall which it did not possess before the war.   In other respects also the position of France is different.   Under the Treaty of Frankfurt, which marked the end of hostilities in 1870, French and Germans were bound to reciprocal most-favoured-nation treatment in perpetuity.   So long as the stipulations of this treaty were in force, a firm basis was given to the most-favoured-nation treaty principle all over Europe. This clause has now disappeared, and in its place has appeared a non-reciprocal most-favoured-nation clause in the Treaty of Versailles, though application of this clause is envisaged for a period of only five years.   Under these circumstances it is difficult to foretell whether the future of the European customs system, based on the practical universality of the most-favoured-nation clause, will be assured to anything like the same extent as happened after 1870.   A further change has occurred as a consequence of the French law of 29 July, 1919, which gives the Government power to negotiate concessions in the general tariff rates of duty, calculated as a percentage of the difference between the general tariff and minimum tariff.   If this law is ever put into application it will practically mean the adoption by France of a treble line of rates, though the general principle of autonomy will still be secured by its application.

Germany did not quite as speedily come under the influence of the economic reaction as France. The moderate *Zollverein* tariff of 1865 (p. 93) became the law of the North-German Confederation, and further remissions were granted in 1868—chiefly affecting cotton, linen, and iron—and again in 1870. In 1873 raw iron was altogether exempted from duty ; and the rates on machinery were at once lowered, with the condition that they were to cease altogether in 1877.

This important series of reforms was evidently due to a desire to copy English economic legislation. The currency, banking, and commercial laws of the new German Empire were closely modelled on the system of the leading commercial state of Europe, with the hope of rivalling her success. The treatment of import duties had the same motive. If England owed her supremacy to her gold standard, her Bank Charter Act, and her free-trade policy, Germany might hope to attain the like position by the same methods, or at least succeed to the vacant place of France in the European economic system.

The endeavour to act on this theory was, however, short-lived. England had other advantages in her progress to commercial greatness than those derived from her policy, and the situation of the German Empire was very different in this respect. The time, too, was unfortunate for bold experiments in economic legislation. The great industrial depression that existed in Central Europe from 1873 to 1879 reduced the profits of business and the receipts of the state. The distress was generally attributed to the absence of sufficient protection against the agricultural products of Russia and America, and the manufactures of England. A new tariff was therefore passed in 1879, in which financial and protectionist aims were combined. A large number of commodities, hitherto free, became subject to duties—iron raw and manufactured, machinery and railway plant, wood for building, horses, cattle, and sheep, also corn and flour. The subsequent steps were very much the same as those already given in the case of France : the corn duties—one mark per 100 kilos (or 6d. per cwt.) on wheat and rye in 1879—were trebled in 1885, and further increased to five marks in 1887. In 1881 flour and some classes of woollen goods were charged more, and up to 1890 the protectionist movement continued.

After 1890 some steps had to be taken to enter into treaty relations, though the Government had to fear the opposition of the agrarian party. What are known as the " Caprivi " Treaties fall into two series, the first concluded in 1891 with Austria-Hungary, Italy, and Belgium, whilst later treaties were concluded with Switzerland in 1892 and Russia in 1894. This last treaty did not come into being, however, before a tariff war had been conducted in 1892.

The treaties thus concluded were to remain in force until 31 December, 1903, and were to be continued thenceforth until denounced. In 1893 also there was a tariff war with Spain ; an agreement was arrived at with the United States in the same year. Later on a tariff war broke out with Canada over the question of inter-imperial preference, which lasted from 1903 till 1910, and in which Canada was, on the whole, the victor. The new tariff was introduced after an elaborate enquiry in the Reichstag in 1901, and was passed in December, 1902. It was marked by a very considerable increase in the degree of specialization and elaboration of tariff schedules. Duties were in general based upon the degree of finish which articles had received, and as a consequence of the powerful position of the agrarian party the power of action of the Government with regard to the reduction of rates of duty on cereals was limited by the inclusion of fixed minimum rates for cereals. Treaties were concluded on the basis of these new general rates in 1904 and 1905 with Belgium, Austria-Hungary, Italy, Rumania, Serbia, and Switzerland. The conventional tariff system came into force at the beginning of 1906 and treaties were to remain in force until 1917. It is extremely difficult to work out the effect of these tariff alterations. Mr. Ashley says that "on the whole the general level does not seem to have been seriously raised." The disastrous termination of the war has very considerably altered the position of Germany. The cession of important territories and the imposition of an enormous indemnity have both crippled the productive powers of the German Republic. At the same time the tariff freedom of the country has been interfered with by a series of provisions in the Treaty of Versailles. Thus it is bound to grant special concessions to goods from Alsace-Lorraine ; but, more important than this, it is bound to accord unlimited non-reciprocal most-favoured-nation treatment to the principal Allied and associated Powers for a period of five years, which may be extended by action of the League of Nations. Under the circumstances the tariff-making policy of Germany is seriously hampered, and it would appear probable that a period of complete autonomy in tariff matters is the only one which could safely be practised by Germany, for it will probably be found difficult for her to obtain concessions from other countries, when these are aware of the fact that any concessions which Germany is in a position to grant to them must be shared automatically by a large number of other countries. The problem of the depreciating mark has been faced by the obligation to pay customs duties in gold.

Italian commercial policy also altered for the worse. From the formation of the kingdom till 1875, as the various commercial treaties and the general tariff of 1861 show, it was liberal and tending towards freedom. About the latter date the forces that we have indicated above as operating generally throughout Europe, commenced to affect Italy. The public expenditure had largely increased, and additional revenue was urgently required. Agriculture was so depressed that, though the country is pre-eminently agricultural, alarm was excited by the supposed danger of foreign competition. The result was that on the general revision of duties in 1877 much higher rates were imposed on the principal imports. The duties on cotton yarns were raised 20%, and for some of the finer goods even 100%. Those on fully-manufactured cottons and linens were increased 50%. Various iron manufactures had to submit to still greater increases, steel rails being particularly selected for taxation in order to encourage their manufacture at home. Soon after the adoption of this general customs law treaties of commerce were concluded with France, and became applicable to England by the " most-favoured-nation " clause.   Depression both in agriculture and elaborative industries continued and strengthened the protectionist party, who succeeded in securing the abandonment of all the commercial treaties, and the enactment of a new tariff in 1887.   As a preliminary, a full inquiry was made by a Commission ; but in spite of a general recognition of the sound principle that taxation should be only for revenue, the practical recommendations, which received the approval of the legislature, were distinctly protectionist. Wheat, flour, sugar, and coffee were placed under higher duties.   Cotton, linen, and iron goods had increases varying from 20% to 200%, according to the quality of the articles, imposed on them.

The first effect of the new system of high taxation with no conventional privileges was to lead to a war of tariffs between France and Italy.   Increased duties on both sides acted immediately on the volume of trade carried on by these neighbouring countries.   A decline in the imports and exports on each side marked the year 1888, which also witnessed a new growth of the contraband trade that had declined under the low duties after 1868.

The formation of new treaties with Austria, Switzerland, and Spain somewhat modified the Italian duties ; they however, remained much higher than formerly.

The Italian tariff of July, 1887, remained with modifications the basis of the Italian customs law until 1910, though the dispute with France was not ended till 1898.   In addition to the treaties already mentioned, treaties were concluded with Germany in 1891 and in 1904, and those with Switzerland and Austria were replaced by fresh treaties in 1904 and 1906 respectively.   In the latter year a treaty was concluded with Rumania, followed by treaties with Serbia and Russia in 1907.   The new tariff contained 472 separate ratings and remained the basis of the Italian tariff system until after the war.   A Committee of Inquiry had been appointed in 1913 to formulate proposals for a new tariff in view of the expiration of the treaties of commerce in 1917.   This Committee reported in 1918, and further committees reviewed the situation in 1920 and 1921. The new tariff, which came into force on 30 June, 1921, and is based fundamentally on the work of the 1913 Commission, has been expanded to cover 953 headings as compared with the 472 in the old tariff, whilst each of the separate headings again contains a very much greater degree of specialization than was the case in the previous tariff. The duties are payable in gold, and, in addition, since the rates are based on the original 1913 proposals for the greater part, the actual rates enforced are subject to increases by the system of adding " coefficients " of duty to bring the rates up to the level rendered necessary by the existing situation, though definitely protective intentions also partly underlie the application of this method, e.g., fostering of new Italian industries.

In Russia the revival (or perhaps it would be more correct to say continued existence) of protection was decisively marked. So early as 1868 some duties had been raised, though others at the same time had been reduced. The war with Turkey was followed by a decree making the customs duties payable in gold ; and as the Russian currency was nominally silver, but really depreciated inconvertible paper, this change was equivalent to an increase of all duties variously estimated at from 30% to 50%, and of course dependent from time to time on the premium on gold. In 1880 duties were raised 10%. The new tariff of 1882 made many duties specific instead of, as formerly, being proportioned to the value, and in 1885 further increases of from 10% to 20% were imposed.

The tendencies to higher protection continued throughout the period which culminated with the outbreak of the Great War, as can be seen from the average rate of duty imposed on imports into Russia. In 1880 these were estimated at 16% on the average ; by 1890 they had risen to 29%, by 1900 they were 32½%, and in 1913 they had fallen somewhat to 28%. This compares with average duties of 7½% in Austria, 8.4% and 8.2% in Germany and France, 9.8% in Italy, and 18¼% in the United States of America, in all cases for the year 1912. A further feature of the Russian tariff was the relatively high rate of duty imposed on raw materials and semi-manufactured articles as compared with the duties imposed on similar commodities in other European states ; these duties in 1912 averaged 22% in the case of Russia as compared with 3% in the case of Germany and France.   In one respect only did the Russian tariff show any advance.   Until 1894 only a single uniform rate of duties was imposed, but from that year onwards a series of customs treaties were concluded, with the result that a second and lower conventional scale of rates came into existence.   The Soviet Government has recently introduced a new customs tariff, so that even in Russia the tendency towards a re-orientation of customs policy has manifested itself.

Spain and Portugal had long been strongholds of protectionist ideas, and the reductions made under the influence of the examples of other countries were not as important as elsewhere, but were continued to a later date— thus the Spanish tariff of 1882 made several reductions. The United Kingdom in particular was excluded from the advantages of the conventional rates in consequence of its supposed unfair privileges to French wines.   This obstacle was fortunately removed, and since 1889 the " most-favoured-nation " treatment was extended to British imports into Spain.   Portugal had yielded the same point some years earlier.

The Spanish era of relative free trade came to an end, however, shortly after 1882.   In 1886 the gradual reduction of duties contemplated in 1882 was suspended, though the era of greater freedom had had a considerable influence on Spanish trade.   Imports had increased since 1867 from 400,000,000 to 941,000,000 pesetas, while exports in the same period had increased from 295,000,000 to 938,000,000. The demand for protection came from the industrials of Catalonia, and the agriculturalists who desired to obtain a monopoly of the home market, in spite of a very large increase in the exports of Spanish wine, which had followed the greater liberty of importation of manufactured articles. A strongly protectionistic Commission of Inquiry had been appointed in 1889, and in 1890 decrees suspending reductions and imposing new agricultural duties were issued.   In

1891 treaties were denounced. In 1892 followed a new tariff, covering 369 against 302 tariff numbers, with minimum duties higher for the greater part than the maximum duties of 1882. Tariff wars followed with France and Germany, and increases in certain respects followed in 1897, 1898, and 1899. A general revision of the tariff took place in 1906. It was ultra-protectionist and very specialized, 697 rubrics being included in the schedules and the rates of duty rising to between 20% and 50% in the case of industrial goods, agricultural products being taxed up to 10%. A further tariff was passed in 1912 ; but Spain, in common with other countries, has found it necessary since the war to revise her customs policy, and after the introduction of a provisional tariff in 1921 a new permanent customs tariff was promulgated in 1922. The provisional tariff of 1921 contained 718 categories. The new definitive tariff, coming into force on 12 February, 1922, contains no less than 1,540. The Spanish customs duties, by a law of 1906, were placed on a gold footing, and at the present time, in addition, the Government has power to impose special rates of duty on articles coming from countries with a depreciated currency.

In Portugal the tariff of 1892 proved to be the logical protectionist sequence of the tariffs of 1861, 1871, 1882, and 1885. The general result was that Portugal was probably the most highly-priced country in Europe so far as articles of prime necessity were concerned. Thus in 1909 it was estimated that wheat was at least twice the price in Portugal that it was outside. The tariff law of 1908 continued these exclusive tendencies, and the result was that a French writer could say that the exclusive tariff policy of Portugal had as its consequence the economic isolation of the country. The law of 1908 was intended to force the hands of foreign countries. It gave power to double duties in the general tariff in cases of discrimination or unfavourable treatment, and allowed the Government to reduce the duties by convention to an extent not exceeding 30% of these general rates. This was followed by an agreement with Germany. In 1910 the Government went still further in its attempt to force the gate open for

Portuguese products, and as a result concluded a convention with France in 1911. A treaty was also concluded with the United Kingdom.

Holland and Belgium have as yet adhered to the system of moderate duties. Next to England they may claim a place as free-trading countries, the duties on manufactures being low. But in spite of the general adherence of Belgium to a free-trade policy, which is forced on the country by her position as a transit area and by the impossibility of her becoming self-sufficing so far as foodstuffs are concerned, the post-war problem of German imports has led to the imposition of special duties on goods coming from Germany. At the same time certain rates of duty were increased, and the law of 10 June, 1920, which has since been extended by various Acts, the latest being dated 30 June, 1922, gave the Government power to increase duties by means of a system of coefficients of increase. In Holland, on the other hand, the protectionists have not been able, in spite of considerable pressure, to induce the country to adopt a series of special measures against Germany, and though the Dutch tariff rates are not as low as they once were, yet Holland, together with Belgium and England, represent centres of relative liberalism as compared with the rest of Europe.

In Switzerland, after a rise in the duties imposed in the tariff of 1888 a new tariff of 1891 still further increased protection, treaties being concluded on the basis of these general rates with Germany, Austria-Hungary, Italy, and other Powers. This tariff remained in force until 1906, a new tariff law having been passed in 1902, coming into force in the year mentioned. The 1902 tariff was very largely based on the tariff desires of the three great associations representing farmers, manufacturers, and traders respectively, these associations having been invited by the Government to state their views on the economic interests of their members. The tariff imposed high duties on foodstuffs, and manufactured articles were taxed 50% higher than in 1891, in certain cases the duties being 100% to 150% greater. At the same time specialization had largely increased, the number of ratings being raised from 476 to 1,164.

The war has had its effect on Swiss tariff policy. The influx of German goods under the stimulus of depreciated rates of duty led to a movement for their exclusion, and the Swiss Government was given powers to this effect. In 1921 also the Federal Council was given power to adapt the 1902 rates to after-war conditions, and to bring new tariffs into operation at their discretion. This was to be done before 30 June, 1923, by which date the Swiss Parliament was to confirm or modify the action taken by the Swiss Council.

A new draft tariff was issued by decree in June, 1921, and a new general tariff was issued on 8 February, 1922, to be applied by decree to products coming from countries which discriminated against Swiss goods or subjected them to particularly high duties.

It is thus very apparent from the course of tariff changes during the last sixty years that the general movement is in the direction of greater restrictions on foreign commerce. The smaller as well as the larger Powers have felt this influence. Even the Scandinavian countries have not been left untouched by the general wave of protectionist sentiment. Thus, in Sweden, after a liberalizing period in the 'fifties and 'sixties of last century, a violent struggle between free-trade and protectionist interests led to a victory of higher protection from 1888 onwards. In that year food duties were introduced. In 1892 protection for manufacturers after the expiration of commercial treaties was carried. In 1895 a further rise of food duties took place. In 1910 a new revision of the Swedish tariff was carried, an increase of duties and a rise in the number of tariff rates from 740 to 1,325 marked the tendency of events. Since the war Sweden also has been considering the possibility of special legislation against German goods. By the end of 1919 a large number of tariff treaties had come to an end and a re-orientation of Swedish tariff policy became necessary. Partial tariff revisions took place between 1919 and 1922, but no general revision has yet been undertaken. In Denmark the last pre-war tariff of 1908 has recently been replaced by a new tariff coming into effect on 1 April, 1922. The general conditions that have led to this state of things have been already noticed, and we have only to notice some further circumstances that are not quite evident, but nevertheless have to be taken into account, in judging of the effects on commerce.

In the first place, it is often said that after all the new tariffs are not so rigorous as those prevailing before 1860 and compare very favourably with the almost prohibitive duties of 1850. As a general statement the assertion is true, though in some cases rates are now higher than ever ; it does not therefore follow that the position of international trade is better than it was. A new economic system has been created in the intervening period, on which even lighter duties have a depressing effect. Commercial transactions at present turn on the attainment of small gains on each exchange, and an additional duty of 5% may destroy this advantage and shut out the particular branch of industry from a former market. As the process of exchange is necessarily double, and involves imports sufficient to balance exports, a check to the export of a product leads indirectly to a reduction of imports and a smaller volume of trade. To compute the total loss that the tariffs of the several European states inflict in this way is impossible, though its amount is beyond question considerable.

As the higher economic development of modern times increases the evil of high protective tariffs, one of the most salient features of that development comes to act in alleviation of the evil. The barriers that high duties build up are speedily broken through by the better facilities of transport. Railways and steamships have reduced the charges on exchange more than recent tariffs have increased them ; the obstacles to commerce are on the whole diminished ; and the amount of trade is growing, as also increasing in complexity and variety. The losses from protective duties are not thereby removed, their pressure is only diminished or rather disguised ; but in their absence the increase of trade would be greater in proportion as they really attain their object.

In another respect such restrictions are more injurious to commerce than ever. Formerly it was limited to articles of high value in proportion to their bulk, and these were usually confined to special regions ; the consequence was that either the duties were purely revenue ones, since there was no competing home production, or they were altogether evaded by means of contraband trade. Now, when cheap and bulky articles are the principal materials of commerce, there is often a home industry of more or less importance, and smuggling on an extensive scale is quite impossible. Silks, fine cloth, rare wines, and spices are much more easily carried, can bear heavier duties, and may be concealed with comparative impunity. Raw cotton and wool, corn, meat, and iron, the staples of modern trade, are strongly contrasted in all these respects. Taxation at apparently moderate rates, added to the cost of transport, is almost prohibitive, and evasion of the charge is hopeless. These articles are, moreover, either auxiliary in the production of more highly-wrought articles, or form the necessaries of the working population ; in either case increase in their cost detrimentally affects industrial development by reducing profits, or, still worse, lowering the labourer's standard of living.

Though the special economic circumstances of a time of transition have led to a general disregard of this injurious operation, it is almost certain that in the future it will command increasing attention.

CHAPTER XI

COLONIAL TARIFFS

THE policy which can be displayed towards dependencies on the part of the metropolitan area can differ very widely, and as a matter of actual fact does differ widely from case to case in the modern world. Nevertheless a tendency towards higher tariffs and greater exclusiveness is a feature of colonial policies everywhere.

We may begin by pointing out certain differences in colonial policies without reference to the actual countries adopting each alternative respectively. Colonies, firstly, may be divided into those possessing and those not possessing self-government in tariff matters. Broadly speaking, it is only within the British Empire that colonial self-government has proceeded very far, and there it is particularly with reference to the group of self-governing dominions, which can nowadays hardly be considered as colonies at all, that the phenomenon of tariff independence shows itself, though signs are not wanting that the right to control the local tariff policy must be granted on an ever-increasing scale, as the case of India abundantly shows.

The distinction just drawn relates to a difference not of *economic* but of *political* status. Whether the colonies have any voice in the framing of their tariffs or not, we may now proceed to draw a distinction between *assimilated* colonies on the one hand and *unassimilated* colonies on the other. In the case of assimilated colonies the tariff *régime* is identical, or as far as possible identical, with that of the metropolitan area, and consequently the logical result of assimilation is complete freedom of intercourse between the colonies themselves and between the colonies and the metropolitan area. In the case of unassimilated colonies

the tariff, whether framed in accordance with local wishes
or not, differs from area to area, i.e. the tariffs of the
metropolitan area and each of the colonies taken separately
are specialized with a view to the needs of the areas themselves.   Non-assimilated colonies may or may not practise
a policy of inter-colonial and inter-imperial free trade or
inter-colonial or inter-imperial preference.

One possible class of unassimilated colonies is that which
falls into the group known as " open-door areas."   The
conception of an " open-door " area is wider than that of a
non-assimilated colony, for areas may be open-door areas
without being colonies.   Open-door areas are those in
which, in consequence of international treaties with a fewer
or larger number of signatories, the tariff *régime* prevents
differentiation between the subjects of one state and the
subjects of another.   Thus, broadly speaking, by a series
of treaties concluded between West European powers,the
United States, and China, the nationals of all the signatory
states are subjected to the same customs duties on importation into China, though, be it noted, China's subjects are
treated differentially.   The class of open-door colony is
found in the equatorial regions of Africa, where some check
has been placed on the ambitions of colonial powers by a
series of treaties, beginning with the Berlin Treaty of 1885,
in consequence of which differentiation as regards duties
is prohibited.   But even here there is to be registered
a decline of free-trade sentiment.   Whereas the original
Berlin Treaty contemplated no import duties at all, and
whereas by an amending treaty of 1890 such duties were
limited to an amount not exceeding a 10% *ad valorem* rate,
by the treaty of Saint Germain-en-Laye of 10 September,
1919, this limitation has been removed, so that although
discrimination is not possible a low-duty *régime* is not
necessarily implied.   It is further to be noted that the
last-mentioned treaty confines the benefit of non-dis-
crimination to members of the League of Nations, and
specifically recognizes the right of each state to grant concessions for the development of the national resources of
the territory over which it exercises domination, and thus
admits of certain abuses in the manipulation of concessions

which, unless carefully watched, destroy the whole value of the open-door principle.

We may sum up, therefore, by saying that the modern world shows three types of colonial tariff policy : assimilated colonies, open-door colonies, and colonies with a special customs *régime* of their own, this last class including the cases of the British self-governing dominions, the tariffs of which show an ever-increasing complexity. In the following pages we will attempt a general survey of the colonial policies of the colonizing powers other than the United Kingdom, and will then treat more specifically of the tariff arrangements within the British Empire.

Two colonizing states, namely, Holland and Belgium, maintain no discrimination of any kind, nor do they practise the policy of assimilation. The territorial possessions of Belgium lie wholly within that portion of Equatorial Africa governed by the Berlin Act of 1885 and its subsequent amendments. The Dutch have since 1872 abandoned differentiation in the whole of their vast colonial empire. We now come to three powers which so far as possible maintain the policy of assimilation. They are Japan, France, and the United States. The Japanese tariff applies for the most part in Korea, Formosa, and Saghalin. Korea was only assimilated in 1920, Formosa and Saghalin in 1909, and free trade existed between Japan and these two areas even before this. Japanese policy is one of assimilation except where international treaties stand in the way, as they do in the case of the " leased territories " in China. In the case of the United States the preamble to the Tariff Act of 1922 states that it is applicable to the United States and all its possessions, with certain exceptions named. This indicates pretty clearly the direction of American policy, though it is true that among the exceptions is the important one of the Philippine Islands and the Virgin Islands, taken over by purchase from Denmark. But American policy shows all the characteristic features which follow logically from the assimilation policy. American goods are admitted free even in the non-assimilated colonies, viz., Philippine Islands and Virgin Islands, as well as the minor possession of Guam. Exports to the United States from the colonies are free except in the case of goods from the Panama Canal zone, which is not regarded as a colony. Inter-colonial trade is reserved for American ships under the Jones Act of 1920, except in the case of the Philippine Islands, where by the Act of 1920 the *régime* of reservation is only applicable after special inquiry by the President. The policy of assimilation in Samoa is limited by open-door treaties which have not yet been fully abrogated. The colonial *régime* of France is very much more complicated than the cases hitherto examined. The basis of French colonial tariff policy is the Tariff Act of 1892, by which assimilation was adopted as the official policy of the French Government. Nevertheless, important unassimilated areas exist, both of the open-door type, such as Morocco and the French possessions in Equatorial Africa, and of the non-open-door type. Among the assimilated colonies are Indo-China, Tunis, Madagascar, certain West-Indian islands, and other areas. This class, therefore, includes some of the most important of the French colonies, even if Algeria is treated, as it usually is, as an integral portion of France. We may sum up the position under the following heads : *Imports into France* are generally free in the case of the assimilated colonies, whilst in the case of the non-assimilated colonies the rates of the minimum tariff are enforced ; but whilst the colonies benefit from the reductions contained in the French tariff of 1910 the increases in the minimum tariff have not been applied to them. French exports *to the colonies* are free, both in the assimilated and in the non-assimilated colonies of the open-door type. *Inter-colonial products* are similarly free in the two cases mentioned.

Foreign products into the colonies are subject to the French schedules, as a general rule, in the assimilated colonies, benefit from the open-door *régime* in certain of the non-assimilated colonies, and are treated according to a special tariff, differing from case to case, in each of the other colonies. Where *export duties* exist they are non-discriminatory. The French colonies are, however, tied to the metropolitan area by the fact that in general to enjoy the benefits of lower duties direct transit is required.

The Tariff Act of 1892 created certain exceptions to the rule that the products of the assimilated colonies should enter France free of duty, the exceptions covering, as a matter of actual fact, the majority of the articles generally known as " colonial products." But these exceptions are now swept away except in the case of sugar, sugar products, and pepper.

A policy of preference but not of assimilation is practised by Italy, Spain, and Portugal. In the case of the Italian colonies there are moderate but increasing duties. There are similarly moderate preferences on the importation of colonial products into Italy. The Italian colonial empire is not a large one, the most important area being Libya, and there tariff preferences were granted from 1914 onwards, though it is asserted that the custom of under-valuing Italian imports for customs duty purposes pro-vided what was virtually a preferential system before that date. The Spanish colonies again are relatively unim-portant. For the greater part they are treated as open-door areas, viz., Morocco, Canary Islands, Melilla, Ceuta. In the case of the Spanish Guinea possessions there are preferences of 50% to 80%, whilst Spanish textiles, shoes, and coal are free of duty. In the same colonies there are preferential export duties ; exports to Spain, if in Spanish vessels, are free, and there is a reduction if exported to Spain in other vessels. There are also certain preferences in the Spanish market to colonial products. The fish, vege-tables, and fruit of the Canaries are free, and there are preferences on most of the important colonial products from the other areas. Goods moving from open-door to non-open-door colonies are treated as foreign goods. In the case of Portugal the general principle is that preference to Portuguese goods must amount to at least 50% of the lowest rate of duty. The same principle is applied to colonial products in the home country and to inter-colonial trade, whilst there are also differential export duties on goods leaving the colonies. Foreign goods re-exported from Portugal to the colonies enjoy in general a preference of 20%. Certain of the colonies are assimilated—Madeira and Azores—though to the general rule of free trade there are certain special exceptions : maize, alcohol, tobacco, sugar. The possessions in the Congo area and in China are open-door areas. Those portions of Portuguese East Africa which are administered by chartered companies are treated in Portugal as being foreign countries, but themselves grant preferences. The other colonies have separate tariffs and separate preferential systems.

The enormous extent of the British Empire and the variety of stages of development which have been reached by various portions of it make a description of the British imperial system very difficult. Certain of the British colonies are open-door areas in virtue of international agreements. In other areas, although the Government is not tied by international conventions, the circumstances of the case dictate a policy of low or no duties, but the tendency in the Empire is towards specialization of tariffs to suit the circumstances of each portion, together with preferences to other portions of the Empire. Any description of the imperial system must commence with an analysis of the situation in the self-governing dominions properly so-called. In Canada, South Africa, and Australia the present position has only been reached after a long process of evolution. These three areas represent vast territories in which internal movement is now free. But this was not always the case. In Australia internal freedom of movement was only gained after the creation of the Commonwealth in 1900. In Canada internal free trade is of very much older date, Canada representing a unified economic system from 1867 onwards, though there were approaches to freer movement before then. In South Africa unity of tariff direction is of even more recent origin. There are no natural obstacles which would serve to carve the country up into distinct economic areas, and consequently a common customs system would seem called for. Even in the days of the South African Republics this was clearly recognized, and the first step towards a consolidation of the South African situation was taken with the conclusion of a customs convention between Cape Colony and the then Orange Free State in 1889. After the South African War a new convention was concluded in May, 1903, and provision was made then for the admission of South African or Central African states into the customs union, but the situation was an unstable one ; the Transvaal threatened to leave the union, and the disputes were only settled after the formation of the Union of South Afiica. Into this customs area certain South African native states under British administration have been admitted, but the position of the Rhodesian territories is not precisely the same as those South African territories which are part of the Union in the political sense. The history of the attempt to create a unified Australian customs area goes back to the very beginnings of Australian history. Already in 1849 the Privy Council's Committee on Trade and Plantations pointed to the desirability of uniformity in the rates of duty, but for many years opposition between the tariff policies of Victoria and New South Wales prevented a settlement of the question.

All the British self-governing dominions are suitable for permanent settlement by the white races. All of them have vast agricultural areas which are by no means fully exploited. Nevertheless, the tendency in all of them is to supplement agriculture by manufacturing developments, only this can fully explain the degree of complexity to which their tariffs have attained, though it must not be overlooked that in all of them the revenue which is derived from tariffs is a very considerable item in the state budget.

The policy of permitting unrestricted or practically unrestricted freedom of action to the self-governing dominions in tariff matters dates historically from the middle years of the nineteenth century. At the present time practically the only limitation which exists on the freedom of the dominions to arrange their tariff matters as best suits them is the rule that a dominion cannot grant to a foreign country discriminatory preferences which the United Kingdom does not enjoy. But in other respects they are perfectly free. They are not obliged to grant preferences to the United Kingdom, and they are not obliged to extend to other portions of the Empire preferences which they have in fact granted to the mother country, nor as a matter of practical fact are the preferential arrangements of the self-governing dominions uniform, though certain administrative aspects of the system of imperial preference show a considerable degree of unity.

The technical form of the tariff in the self-governing dominions differs from case to case. In the case of Canada the basis of the existing tariff law is still the tariff of 1907, although it has been amended from time to time since then. It is divided into eleven groups, which follow very closely the contemporary American division of the subject matter, and these eleven groups contain some 1,213 tariff numbers. It is a little difficult to work out the precise burden of the Canadian tariff. The customs duty per head of the population for the year ending 31 March, 1920 works out at about £4 4s. 6d. ; 35% of the total imports into Canada are duty-free ; the burden of the duty on the remainder varies very much. On wines and spirits the *ad valorem* equivalent is about 53%. On tobacco preparations it is only 6%. On other dutiable merchandise the burden is 22%. If all merchandise, dutiable and free, is considered, the burden works out at about 15% *ad valorem*, and on all dutiable merchandise, exclusive of free merchandise, the duty is equivalent to a 23% rate. Of course, in estimating what the burden of the duty is, it must be borne in mind that certain articles will probably be excluded by the operations of the tariff, so that the total economic effect of any given rate of duty cannot be estimated merely by an inspection of the equivalent *ad valorem* rate. Canada's preferential relationships with the rest of the Empire are conceived on a generous plan. It is necessary to premise that the Canadian tariff of 1907 is a *three-rate tariff*. There is a general tariff, an intermediate tariff, and a British preferential tariff. As a matter of fact, in concluding certain commercial treaties with foreign powers the rates inscribed in the intermediate tariff have in some cases been reduced, so that in estimating the benefit of the Canadian tariff preference to the United Kingdom it is necessary to consider not only the spread between the general and the preferential rates, but also the spread between the preferential and the intermediate rates. Preference was first extended to British products in Canada in 1897, when a flat rate of preference of a quarter of the duty was extended ; but certain articles primarily of importance for revenue purposes were excluded. Under the 1897 Tariff Act certain other portions of the Empire, including New South Wales and British India, were also benefited. In 1900 the preference was made one-third of the total duty otherwise leviable. Between 1900 and 1907 the duty was extended to New Zealand, and South Africa in 1904, British India and the Straits Settlements being other areas also accorded a preference.

In 1907 the Tariff Act of that year greatly changed the system. In the first place, the preference ceased to be a flat-rate preference and became a preference varying from article to article. Next, a large number of separate portions of the Empire were enumerated as entitled to preferential rates, including the West Indies, British Indies, the South African colonies, and New Zealand. It was laid down in the Act that the Governor in Council might withdraw the benefit of the British preferential tariff from a British dominion having previously received it. In 1913 the areas included under the preferential scheme were largely added to ; the remaining South African colonies not already included, the West African colonies and certain Asiatic and American dependencies of the British crown were also included for the first time.

The trade relations of Canada are particularly close with certain of the West Indian islands. In 1913 an Act sanctioning an agreement, known as the West Indian Trade Agreement, by which Canada received certain preferences on Canadian goods exported to the signatory West Indian islands, was passed, and these islands obtained concessions in the Canadian tariff. The products in question were to be dutiable at four-fifths of the rate leviable on similar products from other areas, or at the rates inscribed in the British preferential tariff schedule. This trade agreement has now been replaced by a new trade agreement concluded in June, 1920, by which the preference is made 50% of the rate otherwise leviable, whereas Canadian goods enjoy preferences of 50%, 33⅓%, 25%, or 10% of the rates imposed in various West Indian islands on similar goods imported elsewhere. This agreement is to last for ten years, and is then terminable at twelve months' notice. The United Kingdom enjoys any benefit which might result from the application to her products of the rates embodied in this scheme.

The Australian tariff in its present form came into force on 25 March, 1920. It now resembles the Canadian tariff in being a three-rate tariff; there are sixteen " divisions," and these sixteen " divisions " cover 424 tariff ratings, though the number of articles dutiable is very much larger than this. Australian tariff policy has always been dominated by the fear of the Australian Labour Party that the standard of life of Australian work-men would be imperilled by a too-easy admission of foreign goods ; and Australian tariff policy, as a whole, cannot be gathered from a mere examination of the schedules of the Tariff Act. A complete exposition would require an investigation of the sometimes extremely complicated clauses contained in a series of Acts known as the " Australian Industries Preservation Acts," as well as an examination of the anti-dumping powers of the Australian Government. Australian exclusiveness in trade matters is also noticeable in its preferential arrangements. Apart from the preferences extended to the United Kingdom, Australia grants no general preferences at all, though since 1906 it has maintained reciprocity relationships with South Africa, and has this year (1922) concluded a special reciprocity treaty with New Zealand. The preference to the United Kingdom dates from 1908. At that time it was estimated that out of 251 cases in which preference was given 237 were preferences of 5% and only the remainder were greater than this. It is estimated that in the present tariff, which covers 583 cases of preference, 367 are cases of a 10% preference, 24 are cases of a 12½% preference, 136 are cases of 15% preference, and 32 of a 20% preference. Both the absolute number of preference cases and the absolute amount of the preference are thus very largely increased ; but it must be borne in mind that the absolute height of the Australian tariff has been rising between 1908 and 1920, and it does not follow that the competitive position of the

United Kingdom manufacturers as against Australian manufacturers has benefited in the same proportion as the number of preference cases has gone up. The Australian authorities estimate that in the year ended 30 June, 1920, the customs duty per head of the population worked out at £2 12s. 8d. ; 37% of the merchandise entered free, and the rates of duty on other classes were :—

On wines and spirits, etc., 90%.
On tobacco and preparations, 58%.
On other dutiable merchandise, 18%.
On all merchandise dutiable and free, 14%.
On the total of dutiable merchandise alone, 22%.

Those figures, it is to be noted, do not include the full effect of the increases of 1920.

The present New Zealand tariff dates from the end of last year. It was finally passed on 13 December, 1921. As in the case of Canada and Australia, there are preferential, intermediate, and general tariff rates, the tariff being divided into 14 classes. It is estimated that out of a total number of 644 items into which goods are classified there are preferences to British trade in 427 cases. In the previous tariff there were 483 tariff ratings, and preferences in 208 cases. It is further estimated that the new tariff affects preferentially 85% of the total trade in competitive articles produced in the United Kingdom. The present tariff provides also for the imposing of anti-dumping duties and for the imposition of special duties on goods imported from countries with depreciated currencies. The rates of this special duty vary from $2\frac{1}{2}$% ad valorem in these cases where the depreciation of the currency of the country of origin exceeds 10%, but does not exceed 20% to 25% ad valorem where the degree of depreciation is in excess of 90%. The anti-dumping duties are to be imposed if goods are sold in New Zealand below their selling price in the country of origin, or if they are below their cost of production, or if special concessions in the shape of freight reductions, subsidies, etc., are allowed. The anti-dumping duty is to take the form of a special tax equal to the amount of such bounty or concession, or to the difference between the export price and the selling price or cost of production price respectively. The preferential tariff rates are intended to apply to the British Empire as a whole, including mandatory areas; but the New Zealand Government reserves the right to apply the *general* tariff to goods which are produced in any part of the Empire other than the United Kingdom; and the Act also provides for the application of the intermediate tariff either to imperial goods or to goods the product and manufacture of foreign countries. In addition to maintaining a general preferential scheme, special relations have been maintained with South Africa since 1906. For the year ending 31 December, 1920, the customs revenue per head of the population in New Zealand amounted to £6 5s.; 49% of the imports were free merchandise, and the rates of duty on the goods actually imported were as follow :—

Wines and spirits, 54%.

Tobacco and preparations thereof, 57%.

Other dutiable merchandise, 19%.

On merchandise, dutiable and free, the rate worked out at 12%, and on the total of dutiable merchandise only the rate was 23%. It will be noted that if these figures are compared with those of Australia and Canada there is very little difference in the net burden of customs taxation in all these countries, the average rate on all merchandise being very much the same throughout.

The present South African tariff dates in its main outlines from 1914, though there have been partial revisions in an upward direction since then. The technical form of the tariff is less complicated than that of Canada and Australia; the majority of articles fall into a series of simple " class rates," and there are a relatively small number of articles falling into the classes of special and mixed rates. The South African preferential position is also fairly simple. The British preferential rate is in general equivalent to a 3% reduction on the general rates of duty imposed, but in addition to this preferential rate granted to the United Kingdom the benefits of the lower duties have been extended to Canada since 1904, and to Australia and New Zealand in virtue of special arrangements dating from 1906 and 1907 respectively. Recently, however, relations with Australia have become somewhat strained. South Africa has imposed an anti-dumping duty on wheat coming from Australia. The tendency for an agricultural country to strengthen its economic powers by adding manufacturing industries has been responsible for a sharp rise in protectionist sentiment in South Africa, and this has had its effect on the later amendments to the South African tariff.

One of the remarkable features of the post-war situation has been the rapid extension of the idea of inter-imperial preference in other portions of the Empire. Besides the dominions already mentioned the preference principle in part or in whole has been adopted by the following areas. The concessions extended to Canada under the Canadian-West Indian agreement have been extended to the rest of the Empire by the colony of Trinidad. In Jamaica, by an Act of 1920, preference on cotton piece goods, if the cotton goods are made of imperial-grown cotton, was granted. This has been supplemented by the new tariff coming into force on 8 April, 1922, by which a general preferential scheme, based largely on the terms of the Canadian-West Indian agreement of 1920, has for the first time in the history of the colony been introduced. In addition to certain specific rates of preference on a good many articles, there is a preferential rate of 15% as against 20% in the general tariff on all other articles except those in the free list, and in addition certain British products, including machinery, are free of duty while they are subject to a 5% tariff rate when imported from other areas. These preferences apply only to Canada and the United Kingdom. In 1920, also, an *ad valorem* preference of 2½% or 5% was granted by Malta on a very large number of miscellaneous articles and extended to all parts of the Empire. Similarly by an Act of 4 May, 1920, a preferential scheme very closely resembling the British preferential scheme was initiated by the colony of Cyprus, which granted preferences of one-third or two-thirds on certain selected articles and one-sixth in the case of all other goods. The latest addition to the list of colonies with preferential elements in their tariff schemes is provided by the Fiji Islands. In January, 1922, a new tariff then became effective, introducing, *inter alia*, the principle of preference to all parts of the Empire, the general preferential rate being 12½% *ad valorem*.

The Indian tariff has also in recent years been revised in an upward direction. Whereas in 1917 the general rate of duty was made 7½% *ad valorem*, the general rate of duty is now 11%, whilst a considerable number of articles are dutiable at 20% *ad valorem*. A smaller class of articles are dutiable at 2½%, and there is also a free list. The Indian tariff contains 140 specifications, although some of the tariff numbers include a large variety of commodities, so that the total number of articles dutiable amounts to about 400. In addition to an import schedule there is a differential export duty on hides and skins, and export duties on jute, jute manufactures, rice, and tea. The whole future of the Indian tariff is likely to be very considerably affected by the growing sentiment for Indian protection, in particular against what is regarded as the overwhelming advantage possessed by the more highly developed industry of the United Kingdom, as compared with the somewhat primitive conditions which still largely obtain in India itself.

CHAPTER XII

THE MODERN PROTECTIONIST THEORY

ONE lesson that the study of commercial policy from the historical point of view teaches with the utmost plainness is the dependence of the particular trade regulations adopted by any community rather on the existing social conditions and the interests of the strongest classes, than on any precise theoretical doctrines. It is not by reason of special enlightenment that Manchester and Bordeaux have favoured free trade, nor is it pure want of intelligence that has made Philadelphia and Melbourne strongholds of protection. The great exporting industries everywhere naturally and reasonably desire an extension of their market, while districts that possess special advantages over their countrymen, though not over foreigners, in certain forms of production as naturally though not so reasonably strive to retain the benefits of this superiority.

But though it would be a grave error to regard trade policy as the direct product of theory, there is an inevitable connexion between them. A restrictive commercial system is certain to have a theory of protection as its counterpart, and a free-trade policy will be accompanied by an appropriate doctrine. The function of science is, no doubt, confined to determining the truth or falsehood of propositions; an absurdity does not cease to be such, merely because powerful classes or even whole nations accept it as true. The social sciences are in this respect somewhat exceptionally placed. Dealing as they do with problems in which sentiments and beliefs are often the most powerful factor, they must take account of mistaken views and prejudices, since these errors actually affect the object of study. Thus protection, be it ever justifiable or not, is an existing fact; and has the same claim to full and careful examination as any other fact—say inconvertible paper currency or usury laws—both of which have often been the product of erroneous beliefs as to the means of promoting social welfare.

Economists have, it must be confessed, been a little backward in this part of their work. Of hostile criticism and exposure of fallacies there has been enough, if not more than enough. Exposition of the protectionist standpoint and elucidation of its basis, though at present more needed, are not so easily obtainable.

To understand the position taken up by the modern opponents of free trade, it is above all essential to recognize that the key-note of their system is nationality. The advocates of protection with wearisome repetition set up their plan as national, and contrast it with what they deem to be the cosmopolitanism of Adam Smith and his disciples. The claims of the nation as a whole are accentuated, and regarded as far more important than those of the individual or the world at large. How perfectly this attitude harmonizes with the actual policy of European, and indeed of all protectionist states, is apparent. A particular industry is suffering under the pressure of foreign competition— i.e. a national interest is affected. The state then steps in to protect it against the danger by imposing additional duties on the foreign product, the loss to individual consumers and to the world as a whole being disregarded as unimportant.

Thus regarded, the policy would appear to be nothing but the old mercantile and pre-mercantile methods continued in modern times under a new name. Without denying the portion of truth contained in this statement, we would prefer to dwell on the noteworthy differences in general statement and in special arguments between the older and the now prevalent systems. Those differences may be said to be the outcome of economic discussion and criticism. Up to the middle of the eighteenth century no serious question had arisen respecting the regulation of industry and commerce by the state. Particular measures might be opposed on the ground of expediency, but the broad argument against restraints on commercial activity was entirely unknown. The situation is now completely changed ; for the last hundred years the advocate of protection has had to state his case with constant reference and attention to the free-trade argument. One consequence has been that an unduly large part of protectionist works is occupied by attacks on certain views of Adam Smith or of his successors. Either particular parts of the economic theory of foreign trade are employed, or the plea of exceptional circumstances is put forward as invalidating the general conclusion in favour of liberty. The usual appeals to " practice " against " theory " are due to the same cause. A feeling that economic science furnishes on the whole a basis for free trade is widely prevalent amongst protectionists, who prefer to abandon the science rather than accept what they think is its legitimate result.

The restrictive system, as we might expect, has a distinctive colour, according to the country in which it is expounded. It would be strange if a policy claiming to be specially suited for a particular nation did not bear some mark of that nation's peculiarities. American protectionism is not quite the same as that professed in Germany, and the latter again differs from the position of French or Italian protectionists. There is, however, a general similarity that is far more important than any special divergences, and bears witness to the fundamental unity of the forces that have produced the restrictive policy and belief. Local conditions lead to the elaboration of particular lines of argument, and to emphasis on special points, but the case for protection admits of being reduced to general forms, which are reproduced under the most apparently diverse circumstances.

The earliest advocacy of protection, as distinct from the mercantile doctrine, is probably contained in the *Report on Manufactures* (1791) of the great American statesman, Alexander Hamilton, which, we are told by so hostile a critic as Professor Sumner, " is the best statement of the protectionist argument ever made." Most of the pleas used by Hamilton have been the strong points of the later protectionist schools. One ground urged by him in favour of protection was its adoption by other nations. " If the system of perfect liberty to industry and commerce were the prevailing system of nations, the arguments which

9

dissuade a country in the predicament of the United States from the zealous pursuit of manufactures would doubtless have great force . . . but the system which has been mentioned is far from characterizing the general policy of nations.   In such a position of things the United States cannot exchange with Europe on equal terms."   There is here a distinct statement of the reciprocity or " fair-trade " view, which regards freedom of trade as only serviceable when it is granted by both the trading countries.   As this is a very precarious basis for a policy of protection, since it ceases in respect to commerce with free-trade countries, Hamilton proceeds to develop other reasons for the system of restriction.   To those who maintained that manufactures would arise under the normal action of individual interest, he answers that the initial efforts in this direction will be hindered by " the fear of want of success in untried enter-prises, the intrinsic difficulties of first essays, and the . . . artificial encouragements with which foreign nations second the exertions of their own citizens " ; thus anticipating the " infant industry " argument familiar to readers of J. S. Mill's *Political Ecomony*, and believed by most of them to have originated with him.   The advantages which the establishment of manufactures would bestow are next exhibited.   They are—First, the diversification of industry, allowing of greater division of labour, and " affording greater scope for the diversity of talents."   This plea, which was made for manufactures in a new country like the United States at that time, would equally apply to agri-culture in an old nation such as England.   A second argument is discovered in the statement that additional employment will be given to those not at present in the business, a contention that has even now more popularity than any other of the protectionist pleas.   Third comes the effect of protection in encouraging immigration, by securing new and profitable forms of employment, a point of con-siderable theoretical and practical interest.   Fourthly, the benefit of a more certain and steady market is ascribed to the protective system, which thereby saves the cost involved in the transport of goods.   Since Hamilton's time the advantage of reserving the home market to native producers has been repeated on innumerable occasions by the upholders of the system he favoured. Lastly, he argues that protection, instead of raising, actually *lowers* prices by the home competition that it calls into being, and is thus free from the charge so often brought against it of creating monopolies.

From this very careful statement of the case for protection, Hamilton passes on to consider the mechanism to be employed in a manner that shows most clearly the connexion of his views with the mercantile system. The various expedients that we have seen in action in the seventeenth and eighteenth centuries (Chap. IV) are enumerated, and their relative efficacy considered. Duties on imports, bounties, premiums, drawbacks, prohibition of exports useful for industry, all figure in the list, but are tested with reference to their effect on industry rather than on the influx of money. Since Hamilton was, as Mr. Bourne has shown, acquainted with the writings of Adam Smith, there can be no question as to his position being the outcome of the attacks on the mercantile theory contained in the fourth book of the *Wealth of Nations*. The *Report on Manufactures* is thus a restatement of what its writer regards as the essential truths of the restrictive system, separated from the errors that had furnished a plausible ground of assault on it.

The importance of Hamilton's views does not rest simply on the effect that they produced on American policy, nor on the deservedly great reputation of their author. They have with good reason been regarded as the source from which the two most prominent advocates of protection in the nineteenth century—each of whom succeeded in creating a following—derived their inspiration. List and Carey have each added to and expanded particular parts of the protectionist argument, but the basis of their pleas is to be found in Hamilton's *Report*.

The career of the former—List—was essentially that of an " agitator." In his restless activity and unhappy end he recalls Lassalle, the socialist apostle ; in his persistent advocacy of a particular line of commercial and national policy, he suggests the greater and more honourable name of

Cobden. Born in Suabia in 1789, he entered at an early age into the civil service of his native state ; he soon, however, came in contact with the authorities, and after a short imprisonment went to the United States, where he published (in 1828) a plea for protection, under the title of *A New System of Political Economy*. Returning to Germany in 1832, he became a leader of the protectionist party, and prepared his *National System of Political Economy* that has so profoundly influenced German commercial policy. He died by his own hand in 1846.

The system advocated by List contains the leading ideas that have influenced continental, American, and colonial statesmen in adopting the tariff systems whose history we have traced (Chaps. VIII–X). Starting with the conception that society passes through a series of stages, each of which is an advance on the preceding ones, List holds that the state or governing power can facilitate the process of transition. Omitting the earlier stages of hunting and pastoral life, there are the two distinct conditions of (1) agriculture pure and simple, and (2) of agriculture, manufactures, and commerce combined. It is, or should be, the aim of the statesman to bring his country as soon as possible into the second. Some countries are so backward that this development is at present hopeless for them ; others have already reached it. For either of these the protective system is not desirable. Free trade, on the contrary, is the best policy, as by it the undeveloped countries obtain manufactures that they cannot produce themselves, while manufacturing nations gain a wider market for their products. There is, however, a third group of nations with prosperous agriculture, and ripe for the manufacturing stage. To overcome the difficulties of the transition, protective duties are needed. List believed that the two nations in which he was more particularly interested— Germany and the United States—were in this situation. England, on the other hand, was beyond the need of such expedients, and in her case the maintenance of protection was, he thought, a mistake due to the stupidity of the English governing class. The "industrial protective system" thus appears as an agency to be applied at a special period in a nation's growth ; it is at that stage indispensably necessary for the furtherance of national welfare. In corroboration of his opinion, List makes a persuasive appeal to history, as showing that manufacturing industry has always needed protection as a pre-requisite for its successful development. Italy, the Netherlands, Spain, France, Germany, Russia, and the United States are in turn brought forward to illustrate the proposition that " nations . . . can without inconsistency, and should, change their system in proportion as they advance.   At first, by free trade with nations of higher culture, they emerge from barbarism and improve their agriculture ; then by means of restrictions they give an impulse to manufactures . . . then finally, by a gradual return to the principle of free-trade . . . they maintain the supremacy which they have acquired."   The effect of this argument from past experience has been considerable, both in the United States and on the Continent.

Besides the general statement and its supposed historical justification, List employs several theoretical arguments in support of protection.   The most remarkable is that based on the theory of " productive powers."   Adam Smith and his successors—" the School," as he calls them—confine their attention to actual values, or, in other words, to existing products ; they disregard the capacity to produce those values.   Complete commercial freedom may give the greatest amount of value at a given time, but a wise restrictive policy will increase the production of wealth in the future ;   present loss will in this way be more than recompensed by subsequent gain.   The use of protection is substantially a *national* apprenticeship, and should be judged in that light.

" The School "—to adopt List's phrase—is guilty of other errors ; it deliberately confounds individual with national interest.   Unrestricted exchange is perhaps for the immediate advantage of the exchanging parties, but the transaction that benefits the individual Frenchman and German may not benefit, but rather injure France or Germany.   The American purchaser of imported manufactures, to take another instance, may profit, though the industrial interests of the United States suffer by the check to their development that the purchase of foreign goods causes.

Again, Adam Smith and the economists have failed to recognize the full significance of their favourite doctrine of division of labour. They neglect the increased interchange that the encouragement of manufactures in a hitherto purely agricultural district brings into being. The creation of a " home market " saves the cost of transport, and the increased competition of the new industries lowers prices.

These erroneous doctrines are, in List's opinion, the result partly of the cosmopolitanism which is the characteristic alike of the *Economistes*, of Adam Smith, and of his French and English disciples, partly of their materialistic view of economic life, and partly also of their undue *individualism*, which paid no attention to the existence of nations, and limited unduly the functions of government.

The main contrivance by which full industrial development is to be secured, is the application of protective import duties, varying in amount with circumstances and confined to manufactures, agricultural products and raw materials being altogether exempt. The other expedients are indeed noticed, but receive a very subordinate place.

It is hardly necessary to remark that List's doctrines are a development of those of Hamilton, modified by the national tendency to abstract speculation. The encouragement of manufactures is the common aim ; the advantages to be realized and the mode of obtaining them are similarly conceived. The chief difference is the greater elaboration that List has bestowed on his work, and the use of history as affording confirmation of his assertions.

All that is really suggestive and powerful in protectionist theory can be traced back to Hamilton and List, but before examining the doctrines in detail, some other expositions claim our notice. That of greatest practical weight is found in the writings of H. C. Carey, who for many years carried on a vigorous protectionist propaganda. Commencing his career as a free-trader, he declared himself to have been convinced of the wisdom of interference with exchange in order to shake off the commercial domination of England. "British free trade" was in reality the continuance of the old colonial system. Their greater capital and cheap labour enabled the manufacturers of England to retain the supremacy that protection had originally given them. The remedy, and the only way of reaching true free trade, was by a vigorous use of protection until native industries were strong enough to meet their foreign competitors on equal terms.

The importance of the home market, the advantage that agriculturists gain by the proximity of manufactures, and the necessity of a diversity of industry for a complete national life, are dwelt on by Carey, as previously by Hamilton and List. It cannot be said that there is anything very original in his views, which are wrapped up in a mass of declamation admirably adapted to stir up the national prejudices of his readers. But his influence in creating a so-called school of economists, and thus giving a quasi-scientific colour to the protectionist cause, is undeniable, and should receive due recognition. Like List, he was rather fitted for popular advocacy of doctrines that excited his feelings than for calm discussion of the economic problem of exchange in its effects on the individual and on society.

Germany and America have been the centres where the theory of protection has been most remarkably developed, and in those countries List and Carey are by far the most influential representatives of the policy. Their followers are indeed numerous. Each election campaign in the United States brings out an abundant crop of works establishing to the writer's satisfaction that protection is the mainstay of American industry. The same thing was noticeable when the German tariff of 1902 was under discussion. But by that time it was the danger of "over-industrialization," which was being stressed by the academic supporters of the agrarian interests—notably by men like Prof. A. Wagner, Prof. Pohle, and others. The subject in its commonplace aspects has been indeed, in vulgar phrase, "threshed out," without the addition of much that could strengthen or elucidate the position which we have been considering. Some special arguments have, however, been added which are in complete accordance with the general view that we have taken of the growth of protectionist theory. Just as Hamilton, List, and Carey are, consciously or unconsciously, seeking to repair the breaches in the mercantile system by what they deem more durable material, so are the protectionist theories of Cournot, Bowen, and others adjusted to meet the theory of international trade as taught by Ricardo and J. S. Mill.

The doctrine that exchange always gives a surplus of advantage to be divided in some proportion between the exchangers is so fatal to protection, that its champions are compelled to endeavour to weaken its force, a process usually attempted by summoning up some supposed case in which this result is not reached. These arguments at their best are not so much a defence of protection *as a system*, as pleas for exceptional treatment under peculiar conditions, for which reason we may reserve their consideration for a more suitable place.

Quite different is the situation of some later phases of the protectionist movement that have hardly as yet developed an adequate theory, but which illustrate the influence of actual policy upon economic doctrines, as also the tendency to increased rigour of application that a protective system engenders. The causes already described (Chap. X) that have led to the continental reaction against the liberal policy of 1860–1870, have produced what has not inaptly been called the "system of solid protection." Agriculture and manufactures have both been affected by far-reaching economic changes, and the pressure of public opinion has forced legislators to erect barriers at once against American corn and meat, and against British manufactures. This system, in its essence less reasonable than the system of protection to manufactures simply, is nevertheless far more popular in Europe. The agricultural interest is as determined to secure the aid of duties as the manufacturing one. Whether this policy will survive the temporary conditions that have brought it into being is doubtful, though the difficulty with which the English and French protective systems were reformed in the present century suggests the belief that it will.

Very different circumstances have had a curiously similar effect in the United States. The increases of duties and the criticisms to which they have been subjected are the reasons for the bolder position taken up by the extreme protectionist party, who regard foreign trade as an evil wherever it competes with home production. The protective tariff, with its latest exaggerations, is defended on the ground that American civilization is distinct and separate from that of the world. Its higher standard of comfort can, it is said, be preserved only by complete exclusion of any foreign products that can compete with native labour. This policy of raising a " Chinese wall " around the territory of the United States has received far more support than would at first sight appear possible, and its application undoubtedly involves the employment of protection with respect to all forms of industry.

Colonial protectionist doctrines do not need any special discussion. So far as they are not confined to appeals to experience and the comparative statistics of free-trading and protectionist communities, they do not get beyond a repetition of the arguments already noticed. The need of encouragement to new industries, the advantages of manufactures to the agriculturists themselves, and the special value of the " home market," are the pleas in Australasia and Canada, as in the United States.

The history of the protectionist theories of the present century helps to explain their nature and real origin. In all countries we see that the main idea of their upholders is to secure national development. Wherever we turn—the United States, Germany, Italy, or the colonies—it is the same. To create new industries, to place those struggling into existence on a firmer basis, to secure employment for labour, and to increase population and wealth, such are, in every case, the objects aimed at. Opinions may differ as to the particular objects of encouragement—the followers of List are as much opposed to duties on food and raw materials as the absolute free-trader—but the end to be realized and the general agency to be employed are conceived in the same way.

Another common characteristic of the theories under

consideration is their rejection of the doctrines popularly known in England as " political economy." In their cruder forms they reject altogether the use of general principles and prefer to rely on the practical wisdom of men ; in their more refined developments they take advantage of the many difficulties and complications that such a subject as foreign trade undoubtedly presents. The free trade argument stated by Adam Smith is essentially an appeal to the broad and general advantages of liberty admirably adapted to the spirit of the eighteenth century. Still further popularized, as e.g. by Bastiat and the free-traders of England and America, it failed to comprehend and explain the more difficult parts of the question. The effects of duties on imports are too varied and complicated to be fully explained in a primer or catechism, and the attempt to accomplish this impossible feat supplied the acuter protectionists with a formidable weapon. Cases in which producers suffered from import duties ; examples of industries developed by the aid of protective duties ; conflicts between individual and general interests ; complicated reactions in the distribution of wealth, owing to the effect on the qualities of land in cultivation or the particular situation of labour and capital, were easily discovered, and brought forward as refutations of the free-trade doctrine. Questions that required for their correct solution a knowledge of general economic principles and a capacity for following the course of abstract reasoning, had to be dealt with off-hand and by means of popular discussion. It is not therefore surprising that the effect of such controversies on the ordinary citizen was either to produce a disbelief in the too absolute and unguarded assertions of the free-traders, or at best a feeling that " much might be said on both sides," with the inevitable result of giving full play to the sentiments that in so many societies favour protection.

The theory of restriction has a further advantage ; as presented by its ablest advocates, it is essentially political. Economic doctrines are presented with a temporary isolation and separation of the special element with which they deal, and thereby have gained much in precision and definiteness. But this scientific gain makes them less fitted for immediate application to actual facts. To show that a certain measure promotes or retards the growth of wealth, does not prove it to be beneficial or the reverse ; the other conditions in the problem must be taken into account. The economic analysis is but a single part of the process. Protectionist writings neglect such limitations ; all the considerations that can affect the question are taken into account together ; and though there is an unquestionable loss of accuracy, the effect produced on the reader is probably greater. Broad issues of social progress have far more attractiveness and vital interest than discussions on " the incidence of taxation " or " the distribution of the precious metals." An erroneous or defective economic theory is often accepted as giving a support to useful social doctrines. As Mill remarked half a century ago, " Protectionists often reason extremely ill, but it is an injustice to them to suppose that their protectionist creed rests on nothing superior to an economic blunder ; many of them have been led to it much more by consideration for the higher interests of humanity than by purely economic reasons." The combination of social and economic arguments has given strength to the protectionist belief ; and in order to form a correct judgment, the whole system should be studied, not merely its economic side.

But though the case for restriction does not place its sole dependence on economic reasoning, it is by the nature of the subject compelled to give a good deal of attention to the effects of commercial policy on the production and distribution of wealth. Economic considerations come necessarily to the front, and it is therefore desirable to examine the contentions in favour of restriction primarily from the economic point of view, taking in the social and political results so far as they qualify or limit the results that economic considerations alone would lead to.

CHAPTER XIII

ECONOMIC ARGUMENTS FOR PROTECTION

In arranging the various pleas urged in favour of the protective system, it is desirable to take those that have had
serious influence on policy and that possess real importance,
before noticing contentions that rest on some exploded
fallacy or appeal to vulgar prejudices. A system may fairly
claim to be judged by its strongest positions. Taking this
rule as our guide, we proceed to examine the more important of the arguments, some of which we have already
noticed in considering the general features of protectionism.

I. **Protection aids Young Industries.**—By far the most
effective of the arguments used by the protectionists, as
distinct from those surviving from the days before Adam
Smith, is that which asserts that new industries stand in
need of protection from foreign competition. We have
seen (pp. 129-30) how it was employed by Hamilton, and in
a wider sense by List. For a long period it was the standing
plea of American protectionists ; it has, moreover, received
the qualified approval of J. B. Say and Mill, and is repeated
in numerous German text-books of economics. Stated
shortly, the argument is—The commencement of an industry is beset with difficulties which reach their maximum
when the attempt has to be made in a country hitherto
entirely destitute of anything resembling the particular
form of production. The co-ordination of the various
agents of production into an " establishment " or " factory "
is a process requiring time, and not likely at first to be
remunerative. Besides, in an occupation not previously
known, the supply of labour suited for the industry is at
first wanting. The enterprising manufacturer has to
contend against this and similar obstacles ; on the other
hand, there is no assured market for the product. The

weight of reputation and the advantages that organization and a ready supply of the requisite forms of labour and capital give are on the side of the older producers. But if these initial hindrances could be overcome, it may be that the particular industry would yield its cultivators a satisfactory return. When a sufficient supply of labour is obtainable, and the due amount of organization and " connexion " formed, the occupation may prove to be a valuable part of the national industries.

Such being admittedly the truth, it is very natural to suggest that a protective duty imposed on the product of the industry will give sufficient inducement to native producers to encounter the obstacles in their way, and to establish under cover of this " protection " what will within a limited time become a healthy and self-reliant industry. Here, it may be said, is a case that cannot be set aside by the use of *"doctrinaire* common-places," and which requires sober and careful consideration. The first point to be noted is the *limitation* of the contention. It cannot, as some of the more extreme American protectionists have argued, apply to new industries at any stage of national development, since then these "infants" would need encouragement in the home market. The introducer of new processes must perforce take the chance of loss on himself, otherwise there would be no check on rash and improvident enterprises. To plead for " protection " to new industries in England or the United States involves asking for state aid for all feasible projects. Again, *all* new industries in a new country do not need protection, since many have been introduced successfully without it ; when an enumeration of the successes of encouraged industries is made, it is well to remember the unaided ones that have flourished. The distribution of industries *within* each of the larger countries of the world is a striking witness to the potency of this " natural" extension of business to new areas. It is only so far as there is some special obstacle presented by international boundaries that the agency of protection can be called into operation. Within these comparatively narrow limits the use of protective duties depends on the facts of the particular case. The onus of proof rests with those who advocate their employment, and they are bound to show (1) that the industry to be favoured will after a time be self-supporting, and (2) that the ultimate advantage will exceed the losses incurred during the process. A careful computation of the different elements involved the loss in each year of protection, with interest on the losses during earlier years, the estimated amount of gain to accrue when the time for independence is reached—will, it appears, tend to the belief that protection as an agent for establishing new and profitable industries is not likely to prove satisfactory.   When it is added that the complex and elaborate estimates, which are necessary for a right decision, will have to be made by a legislative body liable to be affected by the influence of interested producers, and at best imperfectly equipped for the task, the risk of trying to encourage by means of protection ought to be sufficiently clear.

Passing from these general considerations to the results of experience, it is interesting to inquire into the actual employment of protection in this respect.   The early industrial history of the United States discloses the remarkable fact that the early development of the cotton, woollen, and iron industries was accomplished with little assistance from duties.   Professor Taussig attributes some efficacy to the tariff of 1816 so far as cotton is concerned, but with this exception, the service rendered by duties was inappreciable, unless the enforced prohibition of trade in the period 1808–1815 (see Chap. VIII) be regarded as such.   The cases of Victoria and New South Wales—the former protectionist, the latter free-trading—are also suggestive.   Without entering on the controverted parts of the comparisons made between these colonies, it may be said that without protection New South Wales had certain manufactures ; while Victoria with it did not much exceed her neighbour in manufacturing development.   " Victoria," said Sir C. Dilke, " makes no linen, weaves no silk, spins no cotton, and manufactures but a small portion of her woollen fabrics " ; though she had protection for twenty-five years for her " infant " industries.

Moreover, the establishment of an industry under cover

of a protective duty does not prove that it is an economic benefit. So long as the duty is continued, there is *prima facie* evidence that it is a loss, and even after it is withdrawn there is much difficulty in deciding whether the gains or losses preponderate ; and if the former do, whether they could not have been obtained on easier terms under freedom. The great complication of the problem, and the natural tendency to favour native industries, make it desirable to insist on applying the most rigorous tests to any particular case. On the whole, the conclusion suggested is that the case of protection to young industries is more a conceivable than practical example of the wisdom of a protective policy. It is akin to those difficult cases that perplex moralists, and belongs rather to the domain of economic casuistry than to subjects fitted for the deliberations of statesmen. What is by its very nature exceptional cannot form the foundation of a general policy.

II. **Protection increases Productive Power.**—The plea that a new industry may stand in need of support against foreign competitors has been expanded into the wider doctrine that protection to industry, while it inflicts a present loss, yet tends to improve the power of the country in which it is applied, and to more than recoup the early losses by the later increase in production. Considered from this point of view, the industrial protective system resembles an investment of capital on the part of the community. Just as it may be in the long run profitable to construct railways that at first scarcely pay their working expenses, or to expend large sums on a system of national education, so, it is argued, there may be ample justification for applying a wide-reaching policy of protection that will bring the nation more rapidly through its several stages of progress, and create the immaterial capital of industrial capacity. The analogy of the individual who expends time and money in learning an art or profession is suggested. National protection is paralleled by the case of the clerk who sacrifices his present earnings to prepare himself for—say, the medical profession.

To deal with this argument fairly, we must concede the possibility of a backward people being improved by the wise direction of a benevolent despotism. A careful and perfectly-organized system of protection might accomplish useful results. The free-trade case, however, rests on the broad and well-established fact that the guidance of individual self-interest is, in purely industrial matters, much safer than the direction of even the best-informed Government. The amount of the national industries will in every country depend on the quantities of labour, capital, and natural agents at the disposal of producers. The effectiveness of production will depend on the distribution of the available forces, and that distribution, depending on so many complicated and disguised conditions, cannot be sufficiently arranged by any state agency. All attainable evidence goes to show that where the ordinary conditions of social life are maintained, the care and interest of those concerned in the work of production are by far the best guarantees for a beneficial employment of the productive resources available. That part of the argument which claims that the power of production is increased by protection—so far as it is distinct from the case of infant industries previously considered—rests on the inadmissible assumption that the interest of the producers will not lead them to take up those industries in which productive power will increase most rapidly. The acquisition of industrial skill is quite as likely to advance under free trade as under protection, though the lines which it takes will probably differ.

III. **Protection is advantageous, as it promotes Diversity of Employment.**—The argument just examined passes very easily into the one now to be considered. From the position that productive power is increased by protection, it is not far to that which maintains that social and even economic advantage results from the possession of a variety of industries. American and Australian protectionists have laid peculiar stress on this part of their case. They show the effects that a town has on the surrounding country ; how it affords a profitable market for agriculturists within its reach, and adds to the value of land. The many ways in which it stimulates intellectual life and promotes culture and civilization are not left unnoticed, from all which it seems to follow that the indefinite and disputable loss that protection inflicts on consumers of imported goods is a small price to pay for such benefits. With a system of pure free trade, new countries would be confined to agriculture and the producing of raw materials, the civilized life that attends manufactures being confined to the older and more settled countries.

To this very effective plea it may be answered that if protection be the price paid for the development of industries and the growth of society, it is not too much for the benefit received ; but there is no proof that such a price is demanded, or that the sacrifice is calculated to secure the desired aim. Whatever may have been the case in earlier periods, there is now no obstacle to the formation of towns and the prosecution of varied industries in new countries. On this, as on other parts of the subject, the conditions of domestic trade throw a good deal of light. The perfect free trade within Great Britain has not prevented the establishment of industries in districts formerly agricultural. American experience is to the same effect. A rude western state is not prevented from gradually developing fresh industries by the absence of protection against its older fellows. The tendency to variation is sufficiently strong to lead to the introduction of suitable forms of manufacture at the earliest moment. The history of industry and commerce is here altogether on the free trade side.

From the economic point of view it may also be urged that mere variety of industry is not of itself desirable. The process of division of labour implies, as its correlative, increasing specialization, which must include the concentration of industries in favourable situations. Thus the cotton industry of Lancashire is preferable to, say, a dozen small and unprosperous industries employing the same number of persons and using an equal amount of capital. The number of industries is of itself no criterion of industrial development, though it is probable that great variety in employment will not be reached in a rude society. The social side of the argument is, however, more important, and however we may question the wisdom of the particular

10

agency of protection, we cannot avoid recognizing the good intentions of many of those who advocate its use for this object.

Though the plea under consideration has been usually made in the interest of manufactures, it can, as we have found (p. 130), be also sometimes used in favour of agriculture. The agricultural depression in the United Kingdom has familiarized us with the cry that the farmer should not be sacrificed to the manufacturer. The growth of the urban as compared with the rural population and the contraction of tillage have suggested fears of the destruction of agriculture, for which protection is, at least, a plausible remedy. To maintain a due proportion between the two great forms of industrial effort, appears to be a problem eminently deserving the attention of the statesman. Here, too, the test of experience seems conclusive. An established industry, or, to speak more correctly, a whole group of industries, is not easily destroyed. More especially in cases where the law of diminishing returns applies, and where a reduced amount of produce can be obtained on cheaper terms, it is almost impossible to dislodge the more favourably-placed producers. A moderate contraction of the wheat area of England would leave no land under that crop that could not compete with the best foreign soil; unless, indeed, it should be required for more profitable crops, when there would be merely a change in the form of cultivation, but on the whole no diminution. In fact, the old rule of letting things right themselves is after all the best.

IV. **Protection encourages Immigration of Labour and Capital.**—Among the arguments that have attracted the more thoughtful supporters of protection this holds a high place. Cournot and Carey have both dwelt on it, and moderate free-traders have conceded the difficulty of dealing with some aspects of the case. The effect of a rigorous protective duty is to shut out the foreign producers of the protected article, who, if they desire to retain their hold on the market, may transfer at least a portion of the industry to the protecting country. Many possible examples of the process have been suggested, from the

Swiss watchmakers brought to France down to the tin-plate workers, whose industry has been affected by American tariffs. A direct increase of labour and capital is gained by the protecting country, and the result is characterized as "the greatest triumph of the protective system" (Roscher). This "victory" is perhaps more apparent than real. To appreciate exactly the effects of protection in this respect, a distinction must be made between the case of a particular industry and industry in general. Where a country is the principal consumer of a commodity—as the United States are, notably, of tin-plates—it is evident that protection, if sufficiently high, will lead to transfer or to the partial abandonment of the industry in other countries. The displaced labour and capital may either change its locality or its occupation, and unless the difficulty of the latter is specially great, this will be the more likely course. But the non-existence of the industry in the protected country proves that the conditions are unfavourable for it; otherwise some beginning of it would have been made. Further, since imports must (other things being equal) balance exports, a part of the protecting country's industry will suffer, unless the transfer takes place at once. The wider effect on the general course of industry is more important. Protection so far raises the cost of living, and thereby reduces both profits and wages; but as high wages and profits are the chief cause of the influx of labour and capital, protection in this way tends to check immigration. In a new country, where interest and wages are both high, this retarding influence may be concealed; but it appears that the great mass of American immigrants are not drawn by protection, since they are not employed in protected industries. The difference between American and English wages is much greater in the case of unskilled than of skilled labour. The often-quoted case of Victoria and New South Wales shows that the movement was from, not to, the protectionist colony. The result is therefore that, while a special industry may receive an increase of numbers through the agency of protection, it has a counter-tendency as regards the whole country by the increased cost of living that it causes. The normal flow of capital and labour to new countries in any case requires no artificial stimulus.

The fear of depopulation or loss of industry through the action of foreign protective systems is, it may be said, wholly unfounded. Switzerland, which was particularly exposed to this risk, has not in fact suffered.

V. **Protection lowers Prices by increasing Home Competition.**—One of the strongest of the free-trade arguments is based on the cost of protection to the consumer. A duty imposed on any commodity raises its price, and thus the expense of supporting the favoured industries is placed on the whole community. Protectionists have sought to escape this result by reference to the effect that increased home production will have on prices. " If," says List, " protective duties enhance for a time the price of domestic manufactures, they secure afterwards lower prices by means of internal competition." If well founded, this would be a complete defence. Lower prices, other things being equal, imply a greater abundance of goods and a better return alike to labourers and capitalists. Unfortunately there is no evidence for the statement that protection lowers prices. The natural course of progress in manufactures tends to reduce their cost of production, and thus there is a downward movement in prices of manufactured goods in all countries, a movement checked, not assisted, by import duties. In the United States the gradual withdrawal of the inconvertible paper currency made the period after the war one of falling prices, a fact that gave apparent force to the argument under notice. A comparison with the scale of prices in other countries brings out the real cause of the change. Besides, the argument really would prove too much, as, if prices were lowered by protection, it would cease to be needed when its full effects were in operation.

VI. **Protection does not raise Prices to the Consumer.**—Very closely connected with the preceding is the plea that the cost of protection is not borne by the consumer. Import duties, it is contended, have to be paid by the foreign producer, and are in fact a toll levied on the privilege of access to the protected market. Profits abroad have to be curtailed, and the national revenue benefits. To fully discuss the truth of this assertion would require a reference to the very intricate question of the incidence of taxation, but for the particular point at issue it is not difficult to see that, granting the assertion, protection ceases to be effective. If, the duty notwithstanding, the foreign supply comes in there is no stimulus to home producers. The sole way in which protection can benefit the native producer, is by raising prices, and if it fails in that its object is unaccomplished. But the view taken of the incidence of these duties is quite incorrect. Taxes on imports can only fall on the producer in the rare case in which there is no second market for the commodity, and there is so little demand for it in the protecting country that the limitation of the supply will not raise the price. Such an instance is hardly a foundation for a general rule.

VII. **Protection secures a Steady Market.**—One of the greatest evils of the modern industrial system is its instability ; prices and wages move up and down in a way that often defies prediction. The price of wheat in England depends, amongst many other things, on the harvest prospects of Canada, India, Russia, and the United States. A temporary remission of the French import duty or the failure of certain winds in India will send up the price in a day. International commerce is more elaborate than the earlier national trade ; therefore any failures or misunderstandings affect the most remote market. A protective policy is sometimes advocated as providing a security against undue disturbance. It appears much easier to gauge the relations of supply and demand in a single country than in the world market that free trade introduces, and therefore the protective system acts as a check on the extending division of labour that the normal conditions of commerce are ever tending to establish (p. 12). This method for preventing fluctuations, however, fails to accomplish its object. Great as are the forces that cause variations in price, there are others that over a large area tend to prevent them. In a widely-supplied market the movements of price depend on a great number of circumstances, but their very number leads to frequent compensation of one by another. The effect of bad harvests in Russia or India may be balanced by a good one in the United States, so that the price of corn may remain steady during a period in which the sources of supply are very different. The very serious element of artificial variations, the result of combination, is less powerful in an open market. " Rings " and " corners " are more likely to flourish with the cover of protection. Both as limiting fluctuations in prices and as tending to correct local inequalities, free trade is decidedly preferable. The possible case of importations to be sold at a loss, or " slaughtered," does not weaken this general conclusion.

VIII. **Protection is advantageous by securing a Near Market.**—We have seen how much stress protectionists lay on the benefits afforded by having a market close at hand. Some of the arguments previously noticed (especially Nos. II and III) have this as one of their aspects. But a more special advantage attributed to a reduction of distance is the saving in the cost of transport. Carey frequently dwells on the absurdity of sending cotton to England and reimporting it in the manufactured state, instead of carrying out all the operations at home. It is plain that the expenditure on transport is a loss to the communities concerned; they would be the richer if this expense could be avoided ; but it ought to be equally plain that the expenditure is not incurred without an object. Transport may be regarded as the final step in production, viz. the placing of goods at the disposal of the consumer. The cost is indeed a deduction from the gains that foreign commerce gives, and when this cost equals the gain the trade ceases. To sacrifice an advantage because it is accompanied by some drawbacks is not a wise or economical course to pursue. The diminution in the cost of carriage that modern inventions have produced, shows how the development of exchange is dependent on facilities for transport. Moreover, the objection would apply with quite as much force to internal trade. If cost of carriage be an objectionable outlay, it is as bad when charged between Chicago and New York as between New York and Liverpool.

IX. **Protection helps to prevent exhaustion of Superior Soils or other Natural Agents.**—This argument, which is chiefly applied to new countries or to those that export raw produce, is deserving of attention.   It appeals at once to economic and to social considerations of very great importance.   In its earlier form it was based on the " earth-butchery " that was said to result from the rude agriculture prevalent in new countries.   The American farmer raised successive crops of wheat without any regard to the drain on the natural fertility of the land that he cultivated.   The export of wheat was in fact an export of part of the fertility of the country.   A protective system that stopped the export was contrary to the immediate interests of the exporters, but in accordance with their permanent economic welfare and that of the community.   The state was bound to take the larger aspects of the question into account, and restrain the selfish action of individuals in order to promote general utility.

The same line of reasoning is still more unreservedly applicable to mineral exports.   The coal of England or the copper of Spain is limited in quantity, and each ton sent abroad leaves less available for the future.   The husbanding of important natural agents is certainly a justifiable policy.   It is much more difficult to show that protection is the proper mode of accomplishing the object in view ; it can only be used with regard to that small part of the products that enter into foreign trade, and it is, further, extremely indirect in its operation.   To impose duties on imported manufactures to stop the export of corn, or on the import of corn to reduce the export of coal, is at best inadequate as a remedy ; nor can we believe that its advocates have much faith in the policy.

X. **Protection checks the Necessity of Recourse to Inferior Soils.**—The preceding argument has naturally suggested the present one.   Soil exhaustion is always disputable, and can be avoided by proper methods of cultivation.   But the continuous export of raw produce is much the same in its effects as an increase of population.   The import of food-stuffs has admittedly the effect of confining cultivation to better soils, lowering prices, and keeping down rents ; the export of such products must have the opposite effect—i.e. it will bring inferior soil into working, raise the price, and increase rents in the exporting country. Some of the strongest reasons for free trade in an old country such as England are thus able to be employed on the other side in countries that export raw produce. The interests of the labourer as a consumer of food become opposed to unrestricted exchange. It is perhaps an obscure consciousness of this fact that leads the more intelligent of the American and colonial artisans to favour protection. While recognizing the truth of the foundation on which this objection to freedom is based, it is at the same time well to remember that it cannot be taken as an isolated fact. The accompanying circumstances deprive it of much of its force. In the first place, the normal growth of population will, independently of free trade, lower the quality of the worst soil cultivated. Again, the increased cost of food is partly compensated by the greater cheapness of imported goods. If the labourer pays more for bread, he pays less for clothes. Another circumstance is also mportant. The necessity of using inferior soils so far reduces the superior advantages of agriculture, and makes it easier to engage in manufactures ; so that those who desire diversity of industry and the formation of a developed society, ought not to object to a process that will lead to the realization of their wishes.

The effect, too, is not all in the one direction ; the law of diminishing returns on which the whole movement depends is operative in a great variety of industries. Even the newest countries import some kinds of raw products. The United States under free trade would probably have no inconsiderable import of agricultural and mineral products, and would so far be benefited, not injured. These several qualifications minimize the weight of what is at first sight a forcible as it certainly is an ingenious argument.

XI. **Protection secures Employment for Labour.**—We have now to pass to a different group of arguments, viz. those that deal with the interests of the working classes. Where political power is widely diffused, it is this side of economic questions that receives most attention. The claims of labour are always kept to the front, and the policy that appears to aim at their satisfaction is sure to be popular. A system that professes to increase employment and provide larger wages for the workers has the strongest hold on the public mind ; consequently the very commonest part of the protectionist case is that it supplies an additional field for labour in the industries that it brings into being. Fresh industries require labour, and this increased demand, as in the case of other commodities, raises its price or wages. Though very persistently repeated, the contention rests on a somewhat easily-exposed fallacy. Whatever theory of wages be adopted, it is certain that the mere existence of an industry under protection will not increase their amount. If wages depend on capital, there is no evidence that the amount of capital will be increased ; if they are measured by the productiveness of industry, protection does not increase the total produce, and therefore does not raise wages ; and even on the popular belief that wages depend on the demand for commodities, protection, though it creates a home demand, shuts out a corresponding foreign demand in the reduction of exports that its operation on imports must lead to. An import of cotton goods or steel rails by the United States gives a demand for corn, meat, or other products to pay the foreign producers of the imports in question. A reference to the primary facts of exchange (Chap. II) suffices to dispose of this argument, which is indeed one of the weakest of protectionist contentions.

XII. **Protection maintains High Wages.**—Next in the present group of arguments is the familiar " pauper-labour " plea. To shut out the competition of cheaper labour is the avowed object of American and colonial protection. The effect of free importation—say the upholders of the restrictive policy—will be to bring down the prices of commodities to the level prevailing in the cheapest country ; but as wages come out of the price of the product, they in all countries must descend to the standard obtaining in the cheapest country—i.e. under free trade American wages would fall to the English, or perhaps the Belgian, or even the Chinese rate ! Those who accept such a view would find it hard to account for the different rates of wages in England, Ireland, and India in the absence of all protection.

But general principles also show the error of the belief. The importation of *goods* will not lower wages ; they can be affected only by the immigration of fresh labourers. A protective tariff that shuts out commodities, while it allows the free entry of foreign labourers, is not contrived in the interest of native workers.

The absurdity of the position can be shown in another way. The staple industries of a country have to export their products at the price obtaining in the market of the world. The farm-hand in the United States gets higher wages than the same class of labourer in England, but the price of the American product is not higher than that of England. The truth is that high wages are the result of superior efficiency of labour, and this is naturally at its maximum in a new country with natural resources not yet fully developed.

XIII. **Protection is rendered necessary by High Wages.**— To contend that protection makes wages high, and then to advocate protection because wages are high, is a rather circular process of reasoning ; but both pleas are brought forward in support of a protective system. The error of the former is, it is hoped, now plain, but there is more truth in the latter. The general productiveness of industry determines whether wages shall be high or low. Some industries are, however, less suited for a country than others. Under freedom such occupations would be abandoned altogether, or contracted to profitable limits. If it is desired to have them on a larger scale, it is necessary that some artificial encouragement should be given. The imposition of a protective duty will probably lead to a higher rate of wages in the protected industries, and enable them to be carried on. The real rate of wages will, on the other hand, be reduced so far as labourers are purchasers from the protected industries, while the total productiveness of the community will suffer through the diversion of labour and capital to comparatively unsuitable uses. That high wages are a bar to the prosecution of some forms of industry is undoubtedly true, but this only shows that there are other and better openings for industrial activity.

XIV. **Home Trade is more Profitable, as it gives double Employment to Capital.**—Readers of Adam Smith will remember the discussion in the *Wealth of Nations* respecting the relative advantage of different uses of capital, and the conclusion that the home trade replaces two distinct capitals, thus differing from foreign trade, which replenishes only one domestic capital. The same line of thought recurs in protectionist writings. The exchange of American corn or cotton for foreign cloth or linen involves only the employment of the capital used in producing the exported cotton or corn. If the exchange had been for American cloth or linen, two capitals would have been replaced, and profits and wages would have been earned by Americans on both parts of the transaction instead of one going to foreign producers. Thus by another road we reach the " home market " argument.

The oversight of those who adopt it is readily apprehended. On home trade there is plainly profit, as it is said, " at both ends," for the simple reason that there has been investment " at both ends " also. Capital and labour can at a given time have only one employment ; the choice lies between producing for home consumption and for export. What is used for one purpose cannot be available for the other. The point to determine is in which wages and profits will be greater. Protection does not of itself increase the amount of productive power ; it, as we have so often noticed, only alters its direction.

XV. **Home is more extensive than Foreign Trade, and therefore the Loss to Producers by lower Prices is greater than the Gain on the small quantity of Imports.**—This case has been illustrated in the following manner. Suppose the total consumption of woollen goods in the United States to be $250,000,000, and that what costs $3 if produced at home could be imported for $2. But with free trade it would be impossible to import so large an amount owing to the difficulty of payment, therefore it is probable that 10% would be imported, the remainder continuing to be produced at home. The fall of price would extend to the whole product, so that the expenditure on woollens would fall to $166,000,000, with very disastrous results to the American producers of woollens. The comparatively small importation would disarrange the whole domestic market.

The foregoing illustration, in order to do justice to it, has been directly taken from an able protectionist writer. That it bears its refutation with it can be readily shown. First, there is no difficulty in importing a larger amount, or in paying for it by the export of commodities; but admitting that there were, it is clear that the price of woollens could not fall unless the conditions of the home industry allowed of its being profitably worked at the lower price. The supposed loss to the woollen manufacturers would mean an equal gain to the consumers, who could employ their $83,000,000 (one-third of $250,000,000) in expenditure on other commodities. As given, the illustration would show that the woollen manufacturers had acquired a monopoly by the aid of protection.

XVI. **Protection prevents an Unfavourable Distribution of Money.**—The old mercantile ideas about the drain of money and the unfavourable balance of trade, the dread of an excess of imports, and the like, having been inherited by our modern protectionists. We need not discuss the cruder forms of the money fallacy, it is sufficient to refer to the general principles of the subject (Chap. III). Some of the more enlightened advocates of protection who reject the vulgar belief in the magical efficacy of money yet claim for the mercantile doctrine a fragment of truth. Though a permanently favourable or unfavourable balance of trade is impossible, there may be a temporary disturbance of the conditions of foreign trade that will necessitate a large export of gold. As the whole system of banking and credit has a stock of the precious metals for its ultimate support, the stability of the system may be, and often has been, endangered by such a call on its resources. When carried beyond a certain point, a monetary drain brings about a commercial crisis with all its attendant losses. More particularly in an agricultural country is there the risk of such a drain destroying the value of the greater part of the national property. To meet the evil, a protective tariff that will reduce importation may be the best remedy. The industrial revulsions in the United States and on the Continent during the first half of the present century are used to support this general argument. The crisis of 1837–1839 was ascribed by Carey to the action of the low tariff of 1832.

The importance of preserving a sufficient reserve cannot be questioned, and a sudden disturbance of the normal balance of imports and exports is likely to produce evil results. A great excess of imports must be paid for at some time, and if the time of payment is delayed, the use of credit for the purpose is not obtained free of charge. Economic forces are sure to act, but their working may injure a great number of persons. The difficulty that besets the use of this fact in support of protection is the absence of any evidence that the evil can be thus remedied. Under any form of commercial policy the amount of imports or of exports may vary, and a sudden drain of money is quite as likely to occur in a protectionist as in a free-trading country. The nature and cure of the economic disease known as a commercial crisis belong to a different part of economics. The most severe crisis and the most protracted depression ever known in the United States were in 1873–1879 under the high war tariff.

XVII. **Protection is expedient in heavily taxed Countries.** —The last of the mainly economic arguments that we need consider is the old plea that heavy taxation makes protection requisite. The weight of taxation in England was a favourite argument in support of the Corn Laws, and at present the burdens of European countries are alleged as a reason for the increase of protection. The grounds on which home taxation is supposed to justify the use of protective duties are somewhat confused. On the one hand there is the idea of equalizing the conditions of competition between home and foreign producers, and on the other the wish to make foreigners contribute to the national exchequer (see No. VI, p. 148). Ought not the foreigner to pay a part of the expenses of the Government whose market he frequents ? The case is thus made to rest partly on economic but also partly on moral grounds. Neither is very convincing. The pressure of protective duties falls mainly on the home consumer, and an additional charge is not the best way of alleviating an already heavy load. The great difficulty of making foreigners contribute to the national revenue, and the certainty that it cannot be accomplished by the use of protection, make it almost superfluous to discuss the question of justice. But it may be remarked that foreign producers have their own taxes to pay, and are not specially benefited by the administration of the country to which they export. The Lancashire cotton manufacturer gains as little from the Government of America as the American farmer from that of England. The pressure of taxation, taken as a whole, may be regarded as the cost of working the national government. This pressure has to be divided among the citizens, and comes from their income. Taxation does not, in fact, form a part of the expenses of production of commodities, except when directly imposed on the article, in which case an equivalent customs duty should be charged on its import.

Such are the chief arguments appealing more or less to economic considerations that have been presented in defence of protection. They have been selected in order to show the strongest points of the system, and with the desire to put them in their best form. Several of the more obvious fallacies have not been mentioned, it being desirable to deal only with such arguments as possess some force or plausibility, and have been adopted by representative protectionists. Two general remarks may perhaps be made respecting those that we have examined. I.—It is not always easy to draw a precise boundary-line between the different heads—e.g. the infant industry argument (No. I) shades off into the plea for development of productive powers (No. II). The encouragement of a steady market (No. VII) is closely akin to the prevention of fluctuations that lead to commercial crises (No. XVI). The grouping is as far as possible based on the principle of putting related arguments together, e.g. the wages arguments (Nos. XI, XII, XIII) are so placed. It is, however, characteristic of wholly or partly fallacious arguments to in this way blend and prevent complete and precise separation. II.—It must have occurred to the reader that the several pleas do not harmonize. That protection lowers prices (No. V) is a statement that can hardly be reconciled with the assertion that it raises money wages (No. XII), or that home producers would be ruined by the falling prices that free trade would cause (No. XVI). Nor can it be reasonably maintained at the same time that protection raises the value of land (No. III) and lowers rent (No. X). These discrepancies are partly due to the existence of different schools of protectionists, who are at variance on such general questions as the law of rent and of population, and thus reach their conclusions from different premises ; but it is still more the result of the position of the protective policy as a popular belief in which contradictory arguments can be combined with little or no sense of their incongruity.

CHAPTER XIV

NON-ECONOMIC ARGUMENTS—POLITICAL AND SOCIAL PROTECTION

THE non-economic side of the protectionist case next claims our attention, and this is often regarded as its stronghold. It is plain that economic arguments pure and simple cannot be decisive. A protectionist may accept the free-trade doctrines so far as wealth alone is concerned, but he may deny that the increase of opulence is the sole or even a principal end of national policy. He may hold, with Adam Smith, " that defence is of much more import- ance than opulence," or his ideal society may be one in which it is not desirable to have great masses of accumu- lated wealth. And this is just as true of the opposite sentiment. A free-trader may think that the economic arguments for protection have a good deal of weight ; he may believe that by protection new industries would be fostered and the stage of manufactures and commerce more speedily reached, and at the same time hesitate to gain these advantages by the instrument of protective duties, with their corrupting effects on politics ; or he may even think that a ruder and poorer state of society is preferable.

Still, on the whole, there can be no doubt that most men regard the increase of wealth as advantageous. It implies greater power over material resources, and greater capacity for dealing with the various evils that beset mankind. We may take for granted that the policy which best promotes the production of wealth is, other things being equal, that to be adopted. The social and political advantages of a policy must be weighed against its economic disadvantages, if such there be ; and the final determination ought to be guided by the result of these calculations. The task is, however, one of extreme difficulty. To estimate the action of a given policy on material progress is not quite a simple matter ; the indirect effects cannot easily be traced and measured ; so many other agencies are at work altering the condition of society and increasing or counteracting the operation of the special force under examination. But the problem is at least a definite one, and attempts at measurement may be made with some approach to probability. The combination of other social ends makes this almost impossible. How shall we balance national security against an increase of wealth ? Or how shall we say that an increase in material comfort is more than a recompense for deterioration in morals ? Or even keeping to things more nearly comparable, what amount of wealth ought to be sacrificed to the attainment of a certain advance in industrial organization ? What, e.g. would be a sufficient price to pay for the acquirement of the factory system ?

The vagueness and indefiniteness of such problems are in a large measure the reason for the division of opinions on the question of free trade and protection. If the discussion were limited to the economic ground, notwithstanding the ingenuity of some of the arguments for special limitations on foreign trade, we believe that the general expediency of the system of free exchange would have been accepted by competent opinion, and have impressed itself on the popular sentiment. The power of appealing from this narrower and more precise issue to the social and political consequences that must always occupy so large a part of the statesman's attention, has been the strongest of the protectionist weapons. Greater room has been given for the influence of sentiments such as national pride and jealousy, for hopes of moral and social improvement by an active policy on the part of the state, and the various economic arguments for protection have seemed to gain in strength from these questionable supports. By a judicious mixture it is possible to prepare a very effective case for those who are desirous of being convinced, and one which has decided attractions for all who do not care for a strict and logical method of reasoning in social matters.

From the very nature of the case it is impossible to classify the non-economic pleas for protection as we have tried to do with these dealing mainly with the economic part of the question. Two great groups can, however, be sufficiently distinguished. We may separate the *political* from the *social*, and deal with each separately.

The foundation of protectionism is, as has been noticed (p. 128), the idea of nationality ; and it is therefore fitting that an appeal to national independence should be one of its main political arguments. The state of war is one of separation from the hostile nation ; all commerce ceases, and so far as each of the belligerents has been previously supplied by the other, it is now compelled to rely on its own resources. Further, one of the most effective of warlike measures is the hindrance of the enemy's commerce either by blockade or by capture of his merchant ships. A protracted state of war may thus force a nation to supply its needs exclusively from its own territory, and if it has previously had widespread commercial relations, the shock and resulting disorganization to the economic system may be very severe and dangerous. Where a large part of the necessaries of life and the raw materials of industry is obtained through foreign trade, the possible evil is at its height. England at present gets three-fourths of its wheat supply from abroad, all its raw cotton, most of its wool, and a great deal of its iron-ore. An absolute closing of commerce would apparently entail starvation, and the Lancashire cotton famine shows the evil of a check to any one large import. Indeed, the greater the advantages of foreign trade the greater will be the loss and suffering from its cessation.

It is this condition that gives force to the protectionist argument under notice. If war may at any time produce such an evil, would it not be wise to take precautions beforehand against such a state of things ever becoming actual ? Economic autonomy is as important a weapon as political energy or military and naval power. The strongest army or the best-equipped fleet will be useless if the supply of food runs short, or if the industrial functions are paralyzed by want of sufficient raw materials. The maxim, " In time of peace prepare for war," will cover the application of protection for the purpose of securing an adequate supply of food and raw materials from the national territory. Such was the best argument in favour of the English Corn Laws. With the experience of the great continental wars (1793–1815) fresh in men's minds, there was some excuse for the effort to make the soil of England supply food for its population. Many of the protective measures of other countries are defended in like manner. Russia, e.g. can urge the need of manufacturing industries to enable her to be independent of German and English importations. The United States claim by protection to have acquired manufacturing industries that relieve them from the necessity of recourse to the English market. A great variety of commodities may seek protection on this ground.

The same sentiment gives support to the idea of a commercial union of the British Empire. Almost every important commodity could be produced within that extensive area in sufficient abundance for the needs of its existing population, and dependence on foreigners would be avoided. The protective duties of the projected *Zollverein* would be an insurance in view of war.

This general argument acquires greater force with regard to the materials used in the conduct of war. A nation that draws its supplies of arms and ammunition from abroad would be ill-prepared to enter on a war with the country from which its supply came, and this case may be extended to ships and their equipment. The instruments of war are beyond question the most essential objects for the sole disposal of the nation, and what contributes to their formation is so far entitled to the same privilege. Such was the reason for the English Navigation Laws, and it was on this ground that they won approval from Adam Smith and J. S. Mill. In the modern world, moreover, these two streams of argument reinforce one another, owing to the character of modern war. War nowadays has been aptly described as a war of materials as well as of men. The whole industrial apparatus reinforces the efforts of the armed forces. Effective preparation for war involves, therefore, the efficient conduct of industries, which, when war actually breaks out, can turn out munitions and equipment. The importance of the chemical industries in this respect gives the demand for their protection a *prima facie* validity, which gains in strength the more likely the chances of war are.

We have endeavoured to state as forcibly as possible the main political argument against freedom of trade. Its importance will plainly vary with the state of society. When wars are frequent and international relations in an undeveloped condition, economic independence is an essential of national life. The whole system of life has to be adjusted to the requirements of warfare, and a policy that checks the growth of foreign commerce and the inter-dependence of nations that is its concomitant appears *prima facie* desirable. But as the need for isolation be-becomes less, and as the industrial activities grow, the wisdom of restriction is less obvious. Even in the seventeenth and eighteenth centuries the advantage of free commerce probably outweighed any loss that a sudden stoppage would cause. For the last hundred years the case for free trade has been steadily gaining ground for, though the technique of war has improved greatly during this period, so has the power of resistance of modern nations. There never was a community less fitted to bear the sudden pressure of isolation than the Confederate States, and yet, though rigorously blockaded by sea and surrounded on land by the far more numerous Northern armies, they were able to carry on hostilities for four years. A nation with a more developed social life would have still greater power of resistance, as the case of Germany abundantly proves. But if it is at all possible for a country to bear up against the effects of war through the stoppage of trade, to hinder that trade in times of peace is undoubtedly inexpedient. It means the inflicting in a minor degree and continuously what produced temporarily by the act of an enemy would be regarded as a serious misfortune.

Moreover, the creation of a large commercial intercourse tends to reduce the chances of war in the future. In any country that exports to another, the exporting merchants and the producers from whom they obtain goods have a strong material interest in the preservation of peace. The countries that supply the United Kingdom with food would suffer by any check to that trade, and those connected with the trade may be counted on as friends to a peaceful settlement of disputes. The extension of international trade thus gives solid guarantees for the maintenance of peace, and is so far a valuable investment quite apart from its direct benefits. A still more important influence is that of neutral countries; to them war means vexatious restraints on their normal trade, but it also, where the previous lines of commerce are closed, affords new opportunities for profit; and, therefore, while the commercial interests of all countries favour peace, they are after the outbreak of war prepared to supply the belligerent whose own trade is most impeded. These are powerful forces, all tending to prevent the exclusion of foreign supplies. Food, as the last war showed, will even in the crisis of war come to England in considerable quantities. We may therefore conclude that a general policy of restriction as a preparation for the privations of war is entirely out of date, while at the same time we recognize the element of truth contained in the protectionist view. It may be said that the course of events has decided the question. A policy of economic isolation is not practicable, while anything short of it would be ineffective. To stop the English trade in corn and cotton would be too evident a piece of folly for any government to attempt it; the best hope lies rather in its increase and in the widening of the area of supply, by which the danger of interruption will be reduced to a minimum.

The impolicy of navigation laws in the present state of economic development is also certain. The carrying trade of the world tends steadily to pass into the hands of those who are willing to conduct it on the cheapest terms. If the trade of any country be confined to its own vessels, there must be so far a sacrifice of advantage that will impede its progress. A measure of legislative restriction cannot call a mercantile marine into existence unless there are other favouring conditions, and with these the chances of growth are better under freedom. What is gained in one direction will be more than lost in another through the enhancement of cost that shipping laws bring about. The repeal of the English Navigation Laws (p. 53) in 1849, though regarded with apprehension by the shipowners, was an aid in the progress of the English marine.

Warlike implements would seem to present an exceptional case, though here also perfect freedom of trade tends to counteract the evils that appear so certain to result. The supply of weapons is now an established industry in several countries, and there is an open market for belligerents in neutral territories, subject to the penalties that contraband trade draws down. In any case, such measures of defence as prudence suggests can be carried out without recourse to protection.

To encourage political isolation might have, at one time, been looked on as a settled rule of statecraft. That France and England were " natural enemies," and that it was desirable to erect barriers between the two countries, formed part of the mercantile creed, and if the goodness of the end be conceded, the method of protection certainly conduces towards it. It was as much on moral and political as on purely economic grounds that Cobden advocated freedom of trade. The tie of material interests would, he felt, lead to a better understanding between nations. Those who desire that harmony should not exist, are therefore correct in suggesting a restrictive policy in order to retard it.

Though such a belief is not consciously professed in any modern country, there is a curious revival of something similar in the extremer protectionist party in the United States. Their position is, however, as much social as political, and furnishes a convenient passage to the discussion of protection as a social agent. The advocacy of protection in America has all along been strongly coloured by anti-British feeling and has had a leaning towards war. Carey, e.g. hardly concealed his belief that a war between England and the United States would be beneficial to the latter, and the earlier protective tariff of 1816 was the direct result of the war of 1812. At present the exclusion of foreign goods is regarded as a mode of forming and maintaining a higher civilization. The old nations of Europe are, it is thought, so different in their environment and organization that it is better to limit carefully the points of contact and allow the new society to expand without the influence of less advanced societies. Protection has thus a social object, to be attained by what is substantially the old idea of political exclusiveness.

Other social aims have also been sought by the aid of protection. The economic argument for diversity of occupation (pp. 144-146) can hardly be separated from the social one. To promote the increase of town populations in new countries, and to raise the standard of culture, has been a primary aim of the more thoughtful protectionists, and has even impressed their critics.

Again, the preservation of an upper class to discharge the political functions that an aristocratic society needs, was a favourite Tory argument for the English protective system. The Corn Laws were in the eyes of many the firmest support of " the Church " and the House of Lords. More limited examples of protection for social ends are duties imposed to cover native producers from the competition of those in other countries where less provision is made for the interest of the workers ; factory laws restrain employers in various ways, and duties to counterbalance their effect on the products of countries where like regulations do not exist, have been proposed on social grounds. Such also was the English differential duty on " slave-grown " sugar that existed for some years before the total repeal of the protection to colonial sugar.

A protectionist policy for the furtherance of social objects does not admit of the same definite measurement as if it were imposed for economic purposes. The onus of proof, however, rests on its supporters ; and they have to make good three separate points, viz., that the object is desirable, that protection will be effectual for the purpose, and finally, that there is no other and better method available. The application of these tests would restrict the use of the particular agency to very narrow limits. Systems that aim at exclusion may be unhesitatingly rejected. With the introduction of steamships, railways, and telegraphs, the possibility of forming a peculiar national civilization came to an end. To expect that the United States can gain any social advantage by shutting out European products is not to be thought of. The interaction of the various nations, in both the material and moral spheres, is the strongest agency of progress in the modern world, as it is one of the most indisputable facts not to be ignored by any wise or prudent policy. The narrower and apparently more reasonable systems that seek to increase either manufactures or agriculture, where one or the other is deficient, are practically in the same difficulty. The general movement that economic forces bring about is not easily controlled. To foster the growth of towns in America or Australasia seems to be a task as superfluous as it is questionable, and on the other hand to restore agriculture to its old preeminence, or even to keep it up to its present extent in old countries, is both difficult and of doubtful expediency.

The most plausible case is perhaps that in which protection is proposed merely as a temporary measure, in order to alleviate the sufferings of producers during a transformation of industry. Most continental countries have employed duties on agricultural produce partly with this object. The loss that a sudden disturbance of economic conditions inflicts is so serious that it may lead to political or social disorder, and the state may have reason to interpose in order to spread the process of change over a longer time. Put in this way, the use of protection appears fully justified, but even here there is a vital condition left out. The duty is imposed ostensibly to give time for adjustment, but its real effect is to encourage persistence in the industry doomed to decline. Instead of taking warning, those employed in it begin to hope for further state favours, so that the requisite change is checked rather than smoothed over. In most cases there is, besides, little need for this artificial cover ; industrial changes are usually spread over a series of years.

Very often it happens that the supposed decline is due to a bad organization of industry, and that foreign competition is the best stimulus to the removal of the defects. Protection has the bad result of removing this natural remedy, and then it simply perpetuates the evil. Antiquated methods of production are continued until perhaps it is too late to effect a change that, carried out at an earlier time, might have preserved the home industry by making it able to meet competition.

Protection, as a set-off against legislative restrictions, is at first sight a carrying out of the free trade principle. Particular excise restrictions are always counted as equiva-lent to so much taxation, and that additional amount is imposed on the foreign product. Factory laws would naturally come under the same class, but in this case the difficulties of a counterbalancing duty are very great. It may be that the regulations in question do not reduce production, inasmuch as they increase the efficiency of the workers. If there is no diminution of production, there can hardly be any ground for compensation for an imagin-ary loss. Again, the real position of foreign industries cannot be accurately ascertained, and will probably be different in each country ; it would, therefore, be necessary to have duties varying according to the country from which the import comes. Then, if a protective duty be just for the home market, equivalent bounties ought to be granted for export ; but the plan of giving, say the English cotton manufacturer, a bounty on export equal to the increase of cost that the English Factory Laws place on him, and making that vary according as the competition that he meets is German, Swiss, or Belgian, may be dis-missed as impracticable. There is, however, a deeper reason against the use of protection for this purpose. Regulations with regard to industry are established in the interest of society. Each occupation has to submit to them as part of the law of the society ; they impose no unjust burden on a particular industry, but are rather designed to prevent injustice. To claim compensation for not doing what the law forbids is not an admissible plea. It may be urged that otherwise the industry will perish, but to this the plain answer is, that unless it can be carried on under the restraints necessary for the well-being of those engaged in it, it is better that it should. The hope that other countries may be led to reform their legislation by the use of protection against their products is a vain one ; they are far more likely to believe that commercial jealousy is at the root of the policy pursued, and to avail themselves of their assumed advantages to the full.

The political and social aspects of the protective policy as just considered do not, taken broadly, add much weight to the case made for it. Allowing that some of the views that it presents are liberal and enlightened, and appeal to the best feelings of the statesman and the ordinary citizen, it at the same time fails to make good its claim to advance the true interests of society. To believe that in any modern state either military power or social progress will be furthered by a restrictive system is not reconcilable with the facts of experience. The balance of probability is in favour of freedom of commerce, even with its inevitable drawbacks in some directions.

CHAPTER XV

THE OTHER EXPEDIENTS OF PROTECTION

DUTIES on imports take so prominent a place in the system of protection that other modes of stimulating national industry have been comparatively neglected, though they may claim a greater antiquity, and have, in many instances, quite as much show of reason. Duties on exports might, for example, prove a most effective encouragement to certain forms of industry. Just as England sought for a long time to retain native wool for her own manufacturers by forbidding its export, so the United States might now restrain the export of cotton and give American producers a considerable advantage. Still, until recently export duties have never been much in favour with protectionists ; the desire of selling as much as possible has been too strong for them ; and the danger of encouraging competitors to seek new sources of supply has been sufficiently realized. The recent revival of the cruder forms of anti-foreign feeling has, however, restored a certain measure of popularity to differential export duties ; for, if by the imposition of an export duty the industries of a rival area are hampered, it may be held that the loss caused to producers of the taxed article can be made up by developments of production in the favoured area. The export duty on hides and skins imposed in India and the short-lived differential duty on palm kernels in West Africa are cases in point.

Somewhat different is the position of another prominent feature of the mercantile system, viz. the employment of bounties on exportation. If it be an object of national policy to increase the amount of exports, nothing can better assist that aim than a payment to exporters ; they will be saved a part of the expense of production, and will naturally send larger amounts abroad, supplying foreigners on cheaper terms, since they are subsidized for so doing. As an encouragement to native industry and a mode of increasing the quantity of exports, the payment of a premium on exports is unquestionably effective, so that if these were the sole ends of the protective policy, it would doubtless be extensively employed. The modern system of protection has, however, a financial as well as an economico-political side. The increase of duties in Europe for the last half-century has, as we saw (p. 96), been partly caused by the needs of governments. Higher customs duties bring in larger sums to the state, and please producers at the same time. There is therefore a double motive for their imposition. A bounty on the other hand drains the public exchequer, and is necessarily limited in its use. To give bounties to a number of important industries would speedily bring about a national bankruptcy or a revolt against the excessive taxation that would have to be levied. There is another hindrance to this special method of assistance. Protection gains a good deal of its popularity from the obscurity that surrounds the operation of import duties. The losses are diffused over the community ; they, it may be thought, fall largely on foreigners, and it requires an effort to conceive the real cost of the policy. But when the amount of support given to the assisted industries appears in the definite form of a grant of public money, opponents can use these figures as the irrefutable basis of their argument that any interference with free exchange is expensive to the society. Still more would this be the case if bounties were granted on production as well as on exportation. American free-traders have often argued that, assuming assistance to be desirable, it ought to be given in this manner, as the nation would then be able to count the cost of the policy, and the real issues would be more easily apprehended. For the same reason protectionists are unwilling to abandon the use of import duties, which command so much popular favour, and are less easily analyzed and tested. The method of bounties is strictly confined to cases where import duties are ineffective, and even in those will be used with much caution and far more readily given up.

One example of the use of bounties is afforded by the shipping industry. Protection to the shipping industry can take a large variety of forms, differing very greatly from one another in the extent to which the protective effect is apparent to the observer or not. If the bounty is given merely in the shape of a mail-packet subsidy, the protective effect depends upon whether the grant in question is or is not greater than the net value of the service which constitutes the theoretical return, and this is obviously a question of fact from case to case. Much more obvious bounties are afforded by bounties on mileage or by bounties upon construction, and as regards these forms of protection a very considerable mass of illustrative material can be instanced. Much attention has been paid to the technique of these bounties by the Austrian professor Grunzel in his book on *Economic Protectionism*, to which the reader is referred for details. Broadly speaking, bounties on building deal with a grant of so much government money per ton, with or without a separate further bounty on machinery, either on the basis of weight (France, Austria), horse-power (Japan), or weight and horse-power (Italy). Again, in France, Italy, and (before the war) Austria, bounties on service were attempted. The simplest form of such a duty is to grant it on the total number of miles run, obviously, but the actual bounties are much more complicated than this. " The generally recognized basis of the bounty came to be the product of the number of tons into the number of miles traversed." A minor question which has arisen has been the question of whether the bounty should be paid on foreign-built as well as on home-built vessels, or whether it should be confined to home-built ships. In France in 1881 half the bounty was given to foreign-built ships, but in 1893 the service bounty was confined to French-built ships. This must necessarily have the effect of enabling the builders of such vessels to exercise a quasi-monopoly, so that part of the gain is transferred to them in the shape of a higher price.

Apart from bounties on construction or for services

rendered, a more direct form of protection to shipping is given by differential duties on imports or the granting of a monopoly to home shipping for certain types of service. Thus it is becoming more and more the practice for coastwise shipping services or inter-colonial shipping rights restricted to ships of the country in question, as is the case with the U.S.A. " Jones " Act of 1920 and the commercial treaties of the latter half of the nineteenth century often excluded coastwise shipping from the conception of " most-favoured-nation " treatment. The prohibition of importation in non-American tariffs, which was a stock element in tariff Acts for many years, though not actually in force, is an example of protection in its purest form.[1]

If the shipping of a country is small relatively to the total volume of work which the import trade of the country requires, the effect of such differential preference to home ships is to raise the cost of imported goods by the amount of the duty imposed. Only in those cases in which the greater part of the goods carried is already carried in ships of the country of import can it be legitimately argued that the foreign exporter will pay the tax.

A further aspect of protection to shipping is afforded by duties of the kind imposed by Spain and France on indirect importation. In France two duties of this kind exist, though their purport is the same. The *surtaxe d'origine* applies to European products imported elsewhere than from the country of origin and the *surtaxe d'entrepôt* to goods not of European origin indirectly imported ; but a certain number of important raw materials have had to be exempted from the dispositions of these taxes. Similarly in Spain the Spanish tariff of 1911 contained a list of surtaxes on certain products of extra-European origin, but imported from a European country either by land or sea. A further development of these taxes on the manner in which goods are imported is afforded by differential duties varying according to the particular frontier over which goods are imported. Thus in the German tariff before

---

[1] The provision was not applicable to goods from countries not insisting on the same right as regards American goods.

1906 several such rates existed, e.g. on salt, certain stones, and hardware. One of the factors which provoked the German-Russian tariff war of 1893 was the fact that the duties on goods imported into Russia varied according as the goods were imported by land or by sea. The late Austro-Hungarian Empire also differentiated between duties on certain colonial products when imported by sea or by land, a factor connected with the struggle of importing interests at Trieste and Hamburg.

The last possible method of differentiating imports is to distinguish between the nationality of importers. This was a feature of English customs duties for many centuries. The duties paid by aliens differed from the duties paid by denizens, but the only example on a large scale existing to-day is afforded by China, where, in consequence of the extra-territorial status enjoyed by the majority of Europeans, the duties paid by these when acting as importers are less than the duties paid by the Chinese themselves. The natural effect, as Mr. Morse, a well-known writer on China, says, is that it leads to an abuse of the flag by unscrupulous foreigners, an effect which was also produced under the old system obtaining in this country.

Possibly the most celebrated instance of bounty legislation in the recent tariff history of the world is afforded by bounties on the production of sugar, which, however, were very largely concealed bounties arising out of the system of excise taxation imposed, coupled with the institution of drawbacks on the exportation of sugar. Since the product was assessed in such a way as to be greater than the amount of the duty which would have been levied on the quantities exported (and this, in view of the type of taxation imposed, it was not always possible to avoid), there was a clear temptation to stimulate the volume of exports. From 1888 onwards a series of conferences attempted to deal with this matter. The United Kingdom for a long time opposed the imposition of " countervailing duties," though a powerful sugar-refining interest in the United Kingdom itself was strongly in favour of this course. The first practical step towards eliminating this constant source of friction was provided by the Brussels Sugar Convention of 1902,

the main principles agreed to being the elimination of all
direct and indirect bounties, the fixing of definite duties on
the import of sugar, and the imposition of anti-bounty
duties in importing countries on sugar coming from non-
signatory states, equal in amount to the amount of the
bounty granted.   The efficacy of this convention was much
weakened by the attitude of the United Kingdom, which,
originally a signatory, agreed to an extension of the convention in 1907 only on condition that it would not be
obliged to impose countervailing duties ; the fact being
that Great Britain, as a large producer of articles in which
sugar is an important raw material, benefits (although its
sugar-producing colonies obviously do not) from any reduction in the price of sugar, however obtained.   The importance of the Brussels Sugar Convention lies, however, partly
in the stimulus it has given to projects for removing
" unfair competition " in other directions.   Thus a considerable stream of opinion has seen in conventions
modelled on the basis of the Brussels Sugar Convention
a solution of the question of dumping, i.e. the sale of goods
at differential prices at home and abroad ; the actual practice of which, or the fear of such practice, being one of the
most potent elements in stimulating protectionist sentiment in the last twenty or thirty years.

One of the most marked features of the last half-century
has been the growth of administrative efficiency.   It is no
longer possible to say, as might have been said in the days
of Adam Smith, that protection would break down on
account of the dishonesty and inefficiency of government.
On the contrary, the efficacy of protection to-day is not
to be measured purely by the rates inscribed in a rate-book.
In comparing protection now with protection in the past,
the effect of improved administrative technique must not
be lost sight of.   The result is that what has become known
as " administrative protection " has acquired in the eyes
of continental protectionists peculiar importance.   Administrative protection is a conscious manipulation of
some of the necessary incidents of importation in a manner
designed to restrict the total volume of goods imported.
Thus veterinary regulations have been used as a means to

exert pressure on exporting areas. The refusal to recognize in the case of articles requiring chemical analyses the certificates of countries it is intended to hamper, the rationing of certain classes of imports, and the use of the power of the state in deciding disputed customs cases, the rigid enforcement of customs regulations in some cases and the turning a blind eye in other cases, are all illustrations in point.

Again, the fact that in the modern world commerce turns very largely upon the use of an international railway net has enabled protectionist countries, by the manipulation of railway rates, to enforce, even more efficaciously than a direct system of protective duties could do, discrimination against the foreigner. Thus, if goods moving between two points are subject to different railway rates if they move in one direction than if they move in another, the inward-moving goods are being subjected to a protective duty. Again, the case already mentioned of the sugar bounty throws light on the use of drawbacks as a protectionist device. It is not in all cases physically possible to measure the direct amount of a taxed material which has been used in manufacturing an exported article, and consequently a margin is given for quasi-protectionist desires to express themselves.

One of the most interesting of such quasi-protectionist devices is the use of import and export certificates, which have not entirely disappeared from France, and which were a feature of German agricultural economy before the war. Owing to the separation of distance between the east and the west of Germany the grain producers of the east found that they could gain more by selling in adjacent areas rather than by selling in the industrial west, where their net income was reduced by the cost of transport, notwithstanding that by selling in the world market they lost the benefit of the agricultural protection which was devised in their interests. Consequently, they pressed for and obtained the right to receive an import certificate which was valid for the free importation of a quantity of grain equal in customs value to the amount they exported. If they then sold their grain in foreign markets, but sold their certificates to importers in the western area who drew wheat from America, for instance, their total income would be equal to the price obtained for these certificates (which were deliberately made transferable in order that they might be sold), and the price realized for their own production of wheat. The effect of this measure on the customs revenue of Germany was very marked. Duties on the importation of wheat are not perhaps at best a very desirable form of revenue, but in the case of Germany the certificate method robbed the corn duties even of this advantage to a very considerable extent. The total customs revenue from protective duties in Germany in 1913 was 440,000,000 marks, but the cost of the import certificates reduced this revenue to 275,000,000 marks.

Among the most sinister aspects of protection in recent years has been the refusal to extend in all cases what has become known as " national treatment." National treatment is the placing of the foreigner for certain or for all purposes on the same footing as the citizens of the country in question. If, then, national treatment is refused, it means that the foreigner is differentiated against in regard to the matters formerly covered by the " national " clause. To realize the importance of such differential treatment in matters concerning trade it is perhaps best to quote the content of one of these " national " clauses in a treaty. Thus, in the case of the treaty between the United Kingdom and Switzerland of 6 September, 1855, the citizens of the two countries were placed on an equal footing in all that relates to the " importation, warehousing, transit, and exportation of articles of lawful commerce." The absence of such a clause might seriously have hampered English merchants in competition with Swiss ones. The outburst of anti-alien feeling which forms one of the most disgraceful aspects of the post-war European situation has unfortunately stimulated the desire on all hands to see further discrimination between citizens and non-citizens of the various trading units.

Political agitations, taking the form of a demand for self-determination, have also had their protective consequences ; in particular, in the conflicts between China and

Japan the use of trade boycotts of Japanese goods has been a marked feature of the situation. In India, also, the boycotting and, in extreme cases, the actual destruction of English goods has shown that unscrupulous manufacturers may find it to their advantage to subsidize such movements, just as American manufacturers may find that the subsidizing of unscrupulous congressmen is a matter of ultimate profit.

The modern protectionist theory is, as we need hardly once more repeat, based on the idea of nationality, and its propounders therefore aim at removing these favours to smaller groups. The utmost freedom of movement, both of services and of commodities, *within* the national territory; rigid protection against all outside competitors; such is, speaking generally, the policy. The system of import duties, bounties, and the other restraints and encouragements is no novelty, but it is in the present age brought into operation with respect to larger and more powerful groups. France, Germany, the United Kingdom, the United States, and Russia are possessed of much greater resources, and permit of a greater amount of free interchange inside their territories than was possible in earlier times. Whether this policy, with its double aspect of external restriction and internal freedom, can be permanent, is a question of the deepest interest, but of its actual vitality there can be no doubt.

CHAPTER XVI

THE PRACTICAL OPERATION OF PROTECTION

AN examination and study of modern commercial policy would not be complete without including some notice of the complications and difficulties that the adoption of a protective system creates. So much of the case for restriction rests on instances of the failure—real or supposed—of free trade in special circumstances, and on rather vague accounts of the advantages that may be gained by a proper regulation of trade, that it is well to see how the protective system works, and what are the embarrassments that result from it. Free-traders are often met by references to the opposition between " theory " and " practice," and to the impossibility of applying an abstract doctrine to the very real facts of trade ; but the truth is that the distinction between " doctrine " and " application " is exactly fitted for the protectionist theory. Granting, for the sake of argument, that a valid defence of protection can be furnished by economic reasoning, it may nevertheless be said that the difficulties of reducing it to reasonable practice are insuperable. A policy suited for the modern world must take account of the general conditions under which it comes into operation, and of the probability that some " friction " may retard movement in the desired direction. It is not protection by itself, but protection with the surrounding circumstances, that has to be studied in order to form an estimate of its probable effects. Some of these difficulties are the necessary result of protection, and are inseparable from it ; others are due to defects of administration, but are so likely to occur that they may be regarded as the natural and probable consequences of the system.

The first result of a policy of restriction that strikes the ordinary observer as undesirable is the increase of cost that it causes. Duties on commodities lead inevitably to a rise of price ; the amount of that rise will of course depend on the rate of duty, and the greater or less disadvantage of the competing native industries. Wherever a protective system has been set up, it sooner or later embraces a larger number of articles in ordinary use by the mass of the people, and makes the conditions of life less satisfactory. If, as is usual in Europe, agricultural products are protected, the necessaries of life become dearer than they would otherwise be, from which it must happen either that the labourers will receive lower real wages, or, if they are so fortunate as to get an increase in their money receipts sufficient to compensate for the higher prices, their employers will suffer by the increased cost of production. But even where food is exempt, or need not be obtained from abroad, duties fall on clothing and the minor articles of consumption in such a way as to affect even the poorest. It is easy to pass over this effect of protective duties with the remark that wages are of more importance to the workers than prices, and that employment is the one thing needed. This view, however, fails to notice that the cost of the labourer's requirements is an essential element in measuring the amount of wages that he gets. No matter what are the other effects of protection, its action in increasing the cost of commodities must always be carefully remembered and taken into account. That protection is injurious to the consumer is a cardinal part of the free-trade position.

The increase of cost through protection is not confined to articles that minister directly to enjoyment. In very many cases the requisites of production are affected. An extensive system of protective duties on imports must fall on various home industries. The elaborate division of labour and the complex organization of industry that modern society exhibits have established very close connexions between different forms of production. What is raw material to one industry is the finished product of another, and a duty granted to the latter is a hindrance to the advance of the former. Duties on cotton, wool, silk, and flax are injurious to the manufacturers of these materials, as, at the next stage of working up, duties on yarns are against the interest of weavers. In like manner protection for iron-ore or coal places the smelter at a disadvantage, and so on through manifold industries. Other and less direct reactions of protection on production may be found. A modern factory is a very complex machine requiring many co-operating conditions for its effective working, from the several classes of raw material that must be obtained, each in due proportion, up to the directing ability and energy of its manager. Any check to the supply of materials, implements, motive power, or labour is a check to efficiency, and diminishes the chance of success. Protection, if largely used, is almost certain to come in as a retarding agency in many industries that are supposed to gain by it. To trace the effects of a duty on a single article, such as coal, all through the industrial area, and see how it operates in hundreds of different employments, where at first sight its influence would never be suspected, is an instructive exercise for the student of commercial policy. The primary effect of protection in retarding consumption is perhaps equalled by its secondary effect in limiting many forms of production.

These effects are both, it may be asserted without hesitation, injurious to the society on which they act; but may yet be believed to be compensated by the advantages of the system, which, by stimulating industry and promoting social progress, confers very great benefits. The whole community thus pays a not unreasonable price for what it obtains. This very comforting belief is dissipated by the fact that industries are unequally affected by the protective action of the state. The distribution of labour and capital and the employment of natural agents follow certain lines under normal conditions. Each country develops the particular applications of productive power in which it has a comparative advantage, and these, it is evident, cannot gain through interference. While the protected industries are in many cases hampered by duties imposed on other products than their own, the great staple trades suffer without any return. Protection can in no way assist the producers of English coal, or cotton goods, French silks, or American wheat; to them it is simply a burden against which their interests will naturally lead them to protest as soon as its real effect is perceived.

These oppositions of interest and the impossibility of any adequate reconciliation are by far the most formidable danger that the protective system has to meet. Consumers as a rule are unorganized, and do not make an effective presentation of their case ; their losses are, besides, diffused over the whole community, and can with difficulty be even approximately estimated. The producer whose raw material is rendered dearer by a duty, or whose market is narrowed by the limitation of foreign trade that protection causes, feels the evil directly, speaks with the weight of practical knowledge, and uses the very kind of argument that is popular with protectionists. The whole policy is in consequence placed in a dilemma from which it is difficult to escape. It must either be applied to all or to very many industries, when its influence in retarding production will be serious, or it may be confined to a smaller number of the more promising cases, when it arouses the hostility of the larger number of unprotected industries. We can thus explain the history of most protective systems. Introduced as tentative efforts to encourage, they are by degrees extended to other industries in order to disarm opposition—an extension which in turn leads to new conflicts of interests, and, perhaps, finally to the downfall of the whole arrangement.

Placed in such circumstances, a tariff to secure acceptance must be the outcome of compromise. Protectionist theory would require either very high protection (amounting to prohibition) all round, or else a careful selection of objects ; its practice is a scale of duties in accordance with the sentiments of the stronger political interests. Small and struggling industries generally come off worst, and the prospects of future development are not properly attended to. The process of give-and-take on which legislation has to be based is not conducive to scientific measurement of consequences or careful adjustment of means to ends.

Closely connected with this difficulty is the risk of inconsistences and anomalies in applying the general idea of protection. To fix the suitable rate of duty on each kind and grade of goods is a problem too hard for the most experienced administrator ; and when the incessant changes in industrial processes, the discovery of new commodities, and the varying relations of trade are added, that difficulty is enormously increased. The first formation and the subsequent modifications of a tariff based on protectionist principles are too difficult a work for anything more than very partial success to be attained, and even this is not often achieved.

Quite as serious, in some respects, is the inconvenience in the work of administration that results from protection. The multiplication of tariff items makes the levying of the proper duties in accordance with law much harder than is desirable. Importers will seek to get their goods rated at the lowest figure : if the duty is specific, by placing them under a low class ; if *ad valorem*, by under-valuation. In the United States, where the protective system has been built up traditionally on an *ad valorem* basis, though this principle has been giving way to specific duties whenever protectionist feeling was strong, as in the last tariff Act, the result of the struggles between importers and the customs officials has been the creation of a complicated quasi-judicial system by means of which disputes as to classification on the one hand, and the proper value to be placed on goods on the other hand, can be settled. The system has gone so far as to require the creation of a special court, known as the " United States Court of Customs Appeals," to crown an intricate series of hearings and re-hearings of classification and valuation cases. The volume of work is very great, and the natural tendency is for the administrative bodies to fall behind in their work. Time is lost, and inducements are offered to traders to evade the regulations, or to search for loop-holes by which their particular goods may escape the ostensible duty. These evils are not simply the result of unskilfulness in devising the necessary measures ; they are rather due to the growing variety of trade transactions and the increased number of commodities to be dealt with.

Protective duties tend unavoidably to encourage efforts

to avoid their payment. Where taxation is purely for revenue, the control of the state is directed to the comparatively small number of industries whose products are taxed so that it can be made effective ; articles to be taxed will be chosen for their fitness in that respect, and the cost will not be excessive. It is otherwise in respect to protective charges. All sorts and qualities of articles have to be made dutiable, and the opportunities for smuggling are increased. In fact, the height to which those duties can be carried depends very much on the inducements that they offer to contraband traders. At periods of exaggerated restriction, as formerly in the case of French trade with England, the smuggler becomes the principal agent for carrying on exchanges.

Such are the difficulties and evils of protection so far as internal trade is considered, but its action on relations with outside markets is still more noteworthy. Industries that require the aid of duties to command a sale at home cannot be expected to meet competition where such support is wanting. By the aid of bounties they may succeed in establishing an export at the cost of the public exchequer, but not otherwise. The vigorous and independent part of the national production which is able to compete with foreigners on equal terms, is checked in its expansion by the increased cost that protection, as we have just seen, imposes, and by the difficulty of carrying on a trade in which return cargoes are not easily obtainable. The doctrine that imports and exports tend to balance may seem a theoretical one, but its truth is brought home to everyone engaged in conducting foreign trade. Thus, as a result of the policy of encouraging native industry, the expansion of one important part of it is materially limited. This effect is propagated over the whole field of industry. The trades that would have gained by increased exports would be in a position to supply capital and business ability for other industries as soon as they became profitable. All the influences of protection have this tendency. Elaborate customs regulations mean loss of time and money, and hinder indirectly the creation of new exports, as they stop directly the growth of imports.

To these economical difficulties in the operation of protection we ought to add the social and political results of placing industry in such direct dependence on legislation. Where the imposition of a duty may make the fortune of a producer or owner of some natural resource, and its withdrawal mean lowered profit or rent, the employer becomes perforce involved in "politics," in the vulgar sense. The English Corn Laws, the French protective system, and the various American tariffs have all been in part the outcome of the exertions of interested parties. Such relations are evil both for industrial and political life, and have a disastrous tendency to demoralize those concerned. It is not well that a matter so vital as the conduct of industry should depend on political contingencies, nor that the work of legislation should be mixed up with questions of commercial loss or gain.

The desire to perfect the technical details of the tariff on the one hand, and to avoid the full effects of the political pressure which interested parties can bring to bear on the administration on the other, has led, especially in the United States, to a demand that " the tariff shall be taken out of politics." At the same time, the idea has gained ground that it is in some manner possible by taking thought to arrive at what has become known as a scientific tariff. In the concrete, these two proposals have merged in the demand for the creation of *ad hoc* bodies or " tariff boards," as they are beginning to be called, in whose hands the consideration of tariff rates shall in the first instance lie, and whose judgment, it is presumed, will be free from party or self-seeking bias. The powers which can be conferred upon such a body can vary very much, from the mere collection of information to the elaboration of tariff schedules. Such a body exists now in the United States, in Australia, and in South Africa, and the tendency of events will force the creation of a similar body in India. It is difficult to take as seriously as the supporters of protection generally do the usefulness of such bodies. So long as they are not endowed with legislative powers their proposals are bound in the long run to undergo the criticism and amendment of the ordinary legislature. In that case, pressure direct and indirect can at once be brought to bear. On the other hand, it is difficult to see how a scientific tariff can ever be arrived at. Tariff-making, in the first instance, involves the expediency of certain principles. On the basis of those principles it is possible with a fair measure of accuracy to adjust means to ends, but the principles themselves are just the ones in dispute, and consequently, although technically the tariff can be improved, acquiescence in the scientific character of the result will only come from those who agree to the fundamental principles upon which the tariff has been constructed. The various tariff boards are in fact placed in the unenviable position of being made finally responsible, in which case they will have to bear the brunt of criticism, and become in fact subject to party dispute, or not being made finally responsible, in which case there is no guarantee that the resulting tariffs will be any the better for the work which they have done.

Again, in its general social bearings, the attempt to bring about an artificial distribution of industry is open to the gravest objection. The industries that receive cover from the state are, by the nature of the case, the least vigorous and the least suited to hold their own in an open market. Instead of the division of employments that natural conditions would lead to, there are either manufactures in countries for which agricultural and other extractive industries are suited, or agriculture maintained to excess where abundant capital and dense population facilitate manufactures. In the former class of cases the tasks of a developed society such as those attendant on the growth of cities are prematurely brought into being ; in the latter the question of the ownership of land, and the relations of employers and employed, are complicated by the increased cost of food and the rise of rent.

All the foregoing considerations are strictly " national " : they relate to the position of the protecting country, and take no account of the world at large. But looking at the matter from this higher and wider point of view, it would appear that the general adoption of the restrictive policy involves a loss to all trading countries. To judge of its extent we must take the system of restriction as it exists, and see how in most nations profitable lines of trade are closed by the action of governments. The lowering of duties by commercial treaties (see Chap. VIII), and the subsequent growth of foreign trade, gives some indication of what the removal of protective duties would do. Without exaggerating the results of such a change, it is not unfair to assume that it would be equal to the advantage gained by the construction of the railway system. In another respect the parallel is appropriate. Protection and distance are both obstacles to commerce, the one natural, the other artificial, and what transport facilities do to remove the one, liberal legislation accomplishes for the other.

Thus by following out the practical operation of the protective system, we see that in economic advantage and in simplicity it is inferior to that of free trade. Looking at the subject in this way, it is scarcely necessary to furnish positive arguments in favour of the latter. We are led to say with Adam Smith that " All systems either of preference or of restraint, therefore, being thus completely taken away, the obvious and simple system of natural liberty establishes itself of its own accord."

CHAPTER XVII

RECIPROCITY AND RETALIATION

MOST Englishmen are disposed to accept the truth of the free-trade principle, if carried out universally. Their difficulty is rather to understand what seems the obstinate persistence of foreigners in a policy of restriction, though in recent years the revival of protection has suggested to many the idea that there must be something in a system that has been deliberately chosen by so many civilized countries, and produced some heart-searchings among those who were formerly satisfied with free trade, or at all events with the prosperity that accompanied it. The preceding chapters of this work have been devoted to an exhibition of this modern tendency, and of the causes that have brought it into being, in the belief that such an inquiry is the most effective way of removing any doubts that may be entertained as to the wisdom of the traditional English commercial policy.

Foreign protectionism has had a further effect on a part of English opinion. It is not uncommon to hear that " free trade all round is very good, but that one-sided free trade is quite the reverse," or that, " as foreigners tax our goods, we ought in turn to tax theirs." The wisdom of unrestricted commerce is believed to be contingent on its adoption by the other parties concerned. Two somewhat different views are, however, often confused : the one which maintains that free trade is bad unless other trading countries accept it ; the other that allows free trade to be good, but asserts that, either to revenge the injuries inflicted by foreign duties on us, or to compel their abandonment, we ought to impose corresponding duties on the goods of protectionist countries. The former is usually described as " Reciprocity," the latter as " Retaliation." Often there is a blending of the two, but in strictness they should be distinguished, as the arguments are not the same and have to be dealt with separately.

The "reciprocity" sentiment is nearer akin to protectionism. It assumes that restriction gives advantages to the nation that employs it, at the cost of still greater injury to foreigners. Of two trading countries each gains by its own protective regulations, but loses still more by those of its neighbour. A removal of restrictions by both parties will be for the interest of both, but should be a matter of arrangement and strictly *reciprocal*. This belief is based on the old idea of trade being gainful only to sellers, but a loss to purchasers. The nations are regarded as being in the same position as individual bargainers, one only of whom is believed to gain by a transaction. The exaggerated importance attributed to the possession of money assisted in the support of this belief. One country would not allow another to draw on its stock of the precious metals by selling goods, unless it received the same privilege in return.

The doctrines of the older system have left deep traces of their existence, and even in free-trade England we need not be surprised to find that the idea of mutual concession is regarded as essential to the success of free commerce. To the creation of this belief, besides the influence of what may be called popular political economy, other elements have contributed. The policy of imposing duties on goods from a country which surrenders that right, and admits everything foreign on equal terms with home products, has an unfair and ungenerous look about it that rouses national feeling. Foreign tariffs undoubtedly injure British trade in some respects ; they close or contract many important markets where profitable transactions would otherwise be carried on, and they are credited with much more power than they really have. Nor have the free-traders themselves been clear of blame in the matter. That other nations would speedily follow the example of England, was the confident prophecy not only of the sanguine and enthusiastic, prominent among whom was Cobden, but of so calm and sober a thinker as John Austin, who declared that in ten years that happy result would be reached. This excessive faith in the power of reason and neglect of the causes that gave so strong a footing to protection, both in new and in backward countries, were perhaps excusable at the time, but they have certainly had unfortunate consequences. Because it was said that free trade in England would be followed by free trade elsewhere, people came to believe that it was desirable on that account, and when the rapid conversion expected did not take place, it seemed as if the measure, having failed of its object, should be given up.

There is of course no doubt that none of the leading advocates of free trade ever thought that its advantage was dependent on its adoption by other countries. Cobden and Villiers have both exposed very clearly the error of reciprocity, but the failure of their predictions on this special matter has notwithstanding gone a long way to discredit the policy to which they were appended. But though it is easy to account for the favour with which the reciprocity argument is received, it must be said that as a guide for policy it is wholly erroneous. The advantages of foreign trade result from the supply of articles on easier terms (Chap. II), and that advantage is realized by the removal of home restrictions. Were the foreign ones to disappear also, the gain would be greater ; but that undeniable fact does not destroy what is obtained by a liberal policy—it is additional to it. Protective duties are impediments on exchange, exactly similar in effect to natural barriers. It would be as wise to argue that British harbours should not be improved unless American ones were similarly treated, as to maintain that England ought not to give up protection unless the United States did so too. An acquaintance with the elementary conditions of foreign trade shows the utter absence of foundation for the belief in the need of reciprocity.

Nor if we follow the argument into details does it gain any additional strength. The fear of an excess of imports, unless the restraint of protection hinders it, can be easily shown to be unfounded. The gain of trade to the community lies in the imports. Corn, meat, cotton, tea, wine, etc., are obtained on cheaper terms, and therefore greater abundance. Such is England's gain by her commerce with other countries, the larger the imports the greater *prima facie* is the benefit. If imports were to come without payment, they would be pure and unmixed gain ; but in fact the relation of imports and exports is, as we saw (Chap. III), governed by definite principles. The proportion between imports and exports is unaffected by the particular commercial policy of a country. Imports have to be paid for by exports, or by a transfer of claims held by the importing country. The transactions of trade are always reciprocal, and no other artificial reciprocity is required.

Another form of this dread of over-importation is that which admits that imports must be paid for, but fancies that the payment will be in money, and will drain the importing country of its cash. The temporary payment for imports by an export of money is not unusual; in such circumstances, the export of gold or silver is the export of a convenient commodity. Over a long period the purchase of imports by export of money is evidently impossible. Not to dwell on the fact, that in a few years the whole metallic stock would disappear, the general range of prices in a country depends, with certain important limitations it is true, on the quantity of money in circulation. The export of money reduces its quantity, and therefore lowers prices ; but lower prices check imports and encourage exports. A transient excess of imports or exports will be speedily corrected by a flow of money from or to the country where the disturbance exists. The alarm on the subject of a money drain has, however, some slight foundation, though reciprocity is of as little use as protection (pp. 156-7) in meeting the difficulty. The true method is banking organization. For, by the appropriate rise in the rate of discount, prices can be made to fall, thus stimulating exports. Where, moreover, the metallic circulation has disappeared, as in Austria to-day, the reason is to be found in a defective currency policy, and has clearly nothing to do with commercial policy. An appeal to experience is probably more effective than any general reasoning in refuting errors as to the relation of imports and exports. Under free trade, English imports have exceeded exports annually for the last forty years, but so for a long time have French imports been larger than exports. At various periods the United States have had larger imports than exports, even with high protection. Similarly with regard to a drain of money. No country has ever permanently been deprived of its currency; compared with the total stock of money, the amount that passes from country to country is insignificant, and its distribution is determined by the requirements of the different nations, and does not need adjustment by the use of duties.

Compelled by criticism to abandon these untenable views, the upholders of reciprocity suggest that excess of imports indicates emigration or consumption of capital. The several thousand millions that had been imported beyond export in the last half-century before the War were looked upon as so much capital gone. It is quite conceivable that a country may be using up its capital, but the state of foreign trade would give no indication of it. The growth of wealth depends on the balance between consumption and production; what remains after supplying the annual expenditure is the net balance for saving. All available evidence goes to show that Great Britain is accumulating capital on a large scale. According to Sir R. Giffen's elaborate and reasoned estimates, the increase in the decade 1865–1875 was from £6,100,000,000 to £8,500,000,000—an increase of £240,000,000 per annum; for the decade 1875–1885 there was a further increase to £10,000,000,000—i.e. £150,000,000 per annum. In 1903 Sir R. Giffen estimated the national capital at £15,000,000,000. Sir R. Giffen's figures have been submitted to sharp criticism, e.g. by Sir J. C. Stamp, but his criticisms affect the absolute, rather than the comparative, value to be placed on them, Sir L. C. Money's estimate was £11,500,000,000 for 1902 and £16,000,000,000 in 1914; Sir J. C. Stamp inclining to the figure of £13,000,000,000 for 1914. Since that time, it is true, the excess of imports has in part been financed by sales of securities and by borrowing, but this was clearly only a temporary episode and the process of accumulation abroad is again going on, as can be best seen from the constant offering of

13

new foreign issues on the London investment market. The great excess of imports has been accompanied by a still larger growth of capital instead of being coincident with its decline.

Another and perhaps more plausible argument for reciprocity is that which assumes that protective duties fall wholly or partly on foreigners, from which it is not unfairly concluded that such duties should be met by corresponding ones. It has already been noticed (p. 148) that this supposed shifting of duties to foreigners is one of the arguments for protection pure and simple, and if it were correct it would furnish a justification of reciprocity. J. S. Mill has sometimes been quoted in support of such a policy, but this is due to an entire misapprehension of his meaning. He, in fact, holds that protective duties are purely mischievous ; and declares that with reference to them, " considerations of reciprocity are quite unessential." Duties for revenue differ in this, and where a foreign country taxes us, we may and ought if possible to tax its citizens. Mill's general view may be accepted, though it requires sundry corrections, but it is confined to the subject of international taxation. If protection be as difficult to apply and as evil in its effects as it has appeared (Chap. XVI), there can be no warrant for taking pattern by those nations that employ it.

Retaliation differs from reciprocity rather in its motives than its method. With those who advocate reciprocity on the ground of unfair treatment by foreigners, the two notions are blended, and their general view has been just considered. But retaliation may be advocated by those who believe that free trade is beneficial, with the aim either of inflicting punishment on other countries for their unwise and injurious policy, or, more frequently, of leading them to " amend their ways," and adopt a more liberal system. As to the first, it need hardly be argued that a nation is unwise in doing what injures itself, even though it may inflict still heavier losses on others. Something might be said in favour of such a course at a time when states sought chiefly to be richer and stronger than their rivals. The *relative* wealth of a community might stand higher by reason of the effects of protection, though its absolute riches were reduced. This way of viewing national prosperity is fortunately discarded, and therefore all justification for a permanent policy of retaliation has disappeared. To keep up protective duties that injure ourselves and our neighbours, as a punishment to them for their unwillingness to become free-traders with sufficient promptitude, is not a policy that can ever win acceptance. Those who have got so far as to see that protection is injurious, will not take long to pass beyond this particular survival of it.

Much more persuasive is the second form of the retaliation doctrine. It allows that protection is evil, but it holds that the temporary loss will receive an abundant return in the benefits of universal free trade. Protective duties may, it is thought, be employed as an instrument of commercial warfare, and like all war, the immediate cost is greater than the returns. Ultimately, however, this relation is reversed ; the objects gained are greater, and repay the earlier expenses. Retaliation, when employed in this way, is analogous to the adoption of protection for immature industries (pp. 140–1.) where there is also immediate loss for the sake of later benefits. It is beyond doubt the most plausible form of the belief, and in Adam Smith's words, " it may sometimes be a matter of deliberation " whether the method should not be employed. If there were a fair probability that the use of protection for a short period would lead to complete free trade, then it may be said that the inconvenience and expense would be amply repaid. To judge, therefore, of the wisdom of retaliation, we have to estimate the chances in favour of its succeeding in the removal of the barriers that it is aimed against. These will, of course, vary in different cases ; the strength of the foreign interests affected by the retaliatory measures and the general disposition of the nations to be coerced or induced first must be taken into account. The problem is, in fact, eminently one for the practical statesman ; but it must be said that there is little evidence of retaliation, or even the milder method of the maintenance of corresponding duties being effective. Nor is it difficult to see why it should be so   The existence of protection in a country

14

shows that the governing classes think that it is good at least for themselves. When they are required by another nation to give up their own policy on peril of retaliation, their faith in it is strengthened, and they not unnaturally fancy that the foreign opposition is due to its success. In addition to its fortifying effect on the protectionist creed, retaliation inevitably irritates national sentiment. Economic legislation is one of the attributes of sovereignty ; a state that cannot deal at its will with its own tariff is deprived of this power, and so far comes under foreign influence, it may be for its good, though excited popular feeling will hardly so regard it. As a mode of securing the progress of free-trade opinions or liberal commercial regulations, retaliation is therefore almost certain to fail. Let us take a particular illustration. Suppose that Great Britain were to attempt a policy of retaliation in order to force the United States into a reversal of their present policy. Is it not as certain as any political event can be that it would be resented as a piece of impertinent dictation, and would lead to a still greater increase of American duties ? Would not it be further said that the use of protective duties for the object of reprisal was in fact a confession by a free-trade nation that its system had failed ? So far from bringing free trade nearer realization, its general adoption would be made still more remote. Such has been the experience of other countries. Canada and the United States have not reached better commercial relations through retaliatory measures. The tariff war between France and Italy is another illustration of their uselessness. The best case for retaliation is where some differential duty is directed against a country that meets it by similar rigour ; but such cases are rare, and are usually settled by negotiation, after great losses have been sustained by both parties to the conflict.

One part of the McKinley Tariff Act brought the idea of what is substantially retaliation into the policy of the United States. Special duties were allowed to be levied on certain articles—tea, coffee, sugar, hides, etc.—coming from countries unfairly taxing United States products.

This reserved power was regarded as useful in negotiating with South American states.   The Tariff Act of 1897 empowers the President to suspend the free entry of certain articles from countries where " unequal duties are imposed on American goods, as also to conclude treaties for a reduction of duties for a limited time, and subject to the consent of Congress."   Whether these provisions can be applied in conjunction with the general system of protection is more than doubtful.   The effort is however interesting, as showing a tendency in American commercial policy, which also was exhibited by England in the period immediately preceding the adoption of free trade.   Very strenuous efforts were made by the Peel administration (1841–1845) to conclude commercial treaties on the basis of reciprocity, but the attempt was a complete failure. Mr. Gladstone, who, as Vice-President of the Board of Trade, had charge of the negotiations, afterwards declared that " In every case we failed.   I am sorry to add my opinion that we did more than fail.   The whole operation seemed to place us in a false position.   Its tendency was to lead countries to regard with jealousy and suspicion, as boons to foreigners, alterations in their laws which, though doubtless of advantage to foreigners, would have been of far greater advantage to their own inhabitants." The lesson thus received conduced to the change of view on the part both of Peel and Mr. Gladstone.

There is, too, an additional reason for the failure both of reciprocity and retaliation.   The views on which they are founded usually arise in developed commercial communities.   England and the Netherlands can both claim the doubtful honour of possessing a fair-trade party. Exporters very soon see the advantage of removing restrictions on trade, but they also feel keenly the hindrances that foreign tariffs cause.   But in such circumstances free trade is so certainly the wisest policy, that it will be finally adopted without reference to the conduct of other countries.   The more refined protectionist position fully recognizes this.   Countries that wish to develop manufacturing industries will not be deterred by threats of retaliation from more advanced nations ;   they will rather welcome any check on their exports of raw produce as helping the progress of manufactures.

This is, in fact, the strongest reason against the use of retaliation by such a country as England. Speaking broadly, and subject to certain exceptions, her imports are food and raw materials ; her exports manufactured articles. Duties to be effective should therefore be imposed on the necessaries of life, or on those of industry, or on both, with the result of injuring the producers, and placing the nation at a disadvantage in its foreign trade. To conclude, retaliation is only likely to be tried in countries that, in List's language, have reached the manufacturing stage. At that stage it is extremely hurtful to the most important industries, and it is altogether ineffective as against communities who seek to create manufactures by the aid of protection. It is consequently doomed to failure as a general method, though in some particular cases it may secure concessions. And what is true of retaliation, also holds good of reciprocity. An offer on the part of France to remove protection if the United States did likewise, would be no inducement to American manufacturers, though unrestricted exchange would be largely beneficial to both countries. Still, when countries are in very different conditions, or in very nearly the same one, there is some prospect of successful arrangements on reciprocal terms. A South American state would find its interest in getting a free market for its raw produce in Europe, and in importing manufactures that it cannot make for itself ; or two countries such as France and England, or Germany and Austria, may be able to agree on reciprocal reductions of duty. Even under these comparatively favourable circumstances, arrangements of the kind are very difficult to manage for the reason indicated by Mr. Gladstone. The policy of pure free trade without reference to the course adopted by other countries is the most consistent, and on the whole, the most effective. When statesmen have got so far as to see the wisdom of reciprocal arrangements, they are not far from the true position, viz. that free trade is beneficial even if it is pursued by a single country.

As retaliation has been advocated against foreign import

duties, so has it been proposed as a means of meeting the other expedients of protection. Duties on exports have sometimes been a reason for heaping additional import duties on the commodity so taxed, with the condition that the import charge shall cease when the foreigner abandons his export duty. Usually, export duties are confined to greatly needed articles, in which case an import duty increases the loss. Still, the reduction of a revenue import duty may lead to the removal of a similar export one, as in the case of currants coming from Greece to England. The export duty is, however, too insignificant a part of the protective system, and has too limited an operation to require much notice.

Foreign bounties are better known, and have at present more practical interest. Whether it is desirable to adopt measures of reprisal against special encouragements to exports cannot be decided until we consider the effect that they produce on the countries to which the export takes place. At first sight it seems well to take advantage of the expenditure of the bounty-giving countries. Most European nations have at some period contributed towards the payment of the English sugar bill, with the result that the consumption of sugar in the British Islands rapidly increased, and far exceeded that of any other country, owing to the lower retail price. Those engaged in the sugar industries, however, complained that they were deprived of profit, and forced to give up their trade in consequence of the state assistance given to their foreign competitors ; they, asked not without plausible ground, for measures to prevent this, or, as they put it, "restore true free trade." The effect of bounties on a particular industry may prove to be serious, and undoubtedly constitutes a " hard case," which could, it would seem, be easily met by the imposition of a duty equal to the bounty. The national exchequer would then receive the grant made by foreign governments to the injury of a class of home producers. This claim of the particular producers, though apparently fair, has yet we believe no real justification. It cannot be said that any body of producers has a vested interest in its business such as would entitle them to protection against competition. Production exists for the sake of consumption ; a duty that countervailed the bounties of other governments is in principle as bad as one that excludes the bounty of nature. If foreign states choose to pay for the export of sugar or other articles, the recipients have no reason to complain. It is, moreover, important to note that the bounties said to have depressed sugar-growers and refiners aided other producers. But, as we have already seen, the Government of this country was for a time of a different opinion (p. 175), though it broke away from the restrictive clauses of the Brussels Sugar Convention in 1907. Moreover, whilst from the economic standpoint there is no very clear line of distinction between a bounty-fed article and a " dumped " article, the policy of adhering to restriction of the latter has lately received the sanction of law.

One argument often urged in favour of retaliation against the bounty system is that which pictures the terrible results of foreign bounties on *all* industries. What, it is asked, would be the fate of the cotton, woollen, linen, and iron manufactures if bounties were to be used in their case ? The rather easily detected fallacy in this argument is the assumption of the possibility of such a case. The cost of the bounties would exhaust the revenues of the countries giving them, while the cheapness to the English consumer, and the increased power of consumption thereby obtained, would more than balance the temporary loss and disturbance. Judged by the test of facts, there is no reason to advocate retaliation as a remedy for the supposed evils of bounties.

CHAPTER XVIII

POST-WAR OUTLOOK AND CONCLUSION

THE tendencies towards protection which were a marked feature of the age of armed peace which culminated in 1914 have, as a matter of hard fact, not diminished since the conclusion of peace. A whole series of factors co-operate to strengthen the reactionary forces in this respect, and the next few years are not likely to show a very considerable diminution in the volume of protection afforded. We must in the first place reckon with the psychological factors involved. The Great War was, from one point of view, the inevitable consequence of nationalistic sentiment, and the length of the war itself contributed to strengthen such feelings. On the tariff side, such sentiments naturally expressed themselves in a desire for the conservation of the national market for national producers, and if this purely instinctive feeling can be reinforced by arguments relating to national safety, the victory for higher tariffs seems almost inevitable. It must be remembered further that the actual dispositions of the treaties of peace are not such as to guarantee a peaceful future. It will consequently always be possible for the argument of national safety to be employed with great effect when revisions of existing tariffs come under discussion.

Two further circumstances require close examination. The war has been enormously more costly than any previous armed conflicts, even if the greatly increased ability to pay of the modern world is taken into account. Consequently there exists on all sides a need for revenue, and though nothing is more completely confirmed by experience than the fact that protective tariffs do not produce a revenue substantially larger than would be produced by a free-trade tariff, except at the expense of the standard of living of the great mass of the population, nevertheless this argument has never penetrated fully into the popular mind, and the result is that high tariffs can always be defended by reference to the overwhelming need for the balancing of budgets.

The need for revenue is certainly overwhelming, but the use of tariff measures as an instrument of taxation is reinforced by circumstances relating to the currency and price situation over parts of Europe. In consequence of limitless inflation prices have risen enormously. In consequence of the fact that the technical method of levying duties which tended to be more and more adopted in European tariffs was the method of levying specific duties, the rates actually imposed took very little account of rising and falling prices. A sharp fall in the price level, so long as specific duties are levied, involves an increased burden of taxation; but the higher and the sharper prices rise, the smaller is the net burden of taxation imposed by a given rate of duty. So long as these price changes were relatively mild and spread over considerable periods of time, it was possible to maintain a relatively stable tax system without influencing too much the net degree of protection afforded, but the post-war situation offered examples of price rises of quite unsuspected magnitude and rapidity. It was consequently necessary to revise the specific rates of duty in an upward direction, merely to keep pace with the rising level of prices. This was accomplished in France and Belgium by the device of the so-called "coefficients," i.e. the rates of duty inscribed in the tariff were subjected to multiplication by given indices, which could be varied as the price level rose or fell. Where the rise in the price level was clearly to be ascribed to monetary inflation the simplest method of adjusting the rates of taxation to the new situation was by demanding the payment of customs duties in gold, and over the whole of Central and Eastern Europe to-day the duties payable are demanded in gold, i.e. the duties are actually paid in paper but at a rate which varies with the premium on gold expressed in terms of the local currency. Such measures, it is to be noted, do not increase the substantial measure of protection afforded, but readjust it to the altered price situation of the countries concerned.

We now come to a further circumstance connected with the currency situation. It has already been pointed out in previous chapters that the fear of " dumping " was a potent factor in producing a demand for protection. Owing, however, to the phenomenon first scientifically investigated in the last few years, of currencies possessing a varying purchasing power inside and outside the country, the world is faced to-day with the phenomenon of " exchange dumping," and a series of measures in England, Spain, Switzerland, Australia, and elsewhere have been devised for the purpose of preventing an influx of goods promoted by the phenomenon in question. The validity of such measures may very well be questioned. The solution of the difficulty of " exchange dumping " lies in a reorganization and restabilization of the currency situation in Central Europe. It is further extremely doubtful whether the magnitude of such dumping is as great as it is popularly supposed to be, since the efforts at any rate of the German Government—and it is Germany which primarily comes into question here—have been consistently directed towards selling goods abroad in terms of foreign currency and at prices considerably above those ruling in the domestic market, by the devices of export taxes designed to bridge the gap between the external and internal value of the mark, of encouraging " invoicing " in foreign currencies and insisting on a rigid system of export licensing. Nevertheless the fear of such exchange dumping has been a potent instrument in producing not only special devices and strengthening the demand for general prohibition, but of contributing a further element of unrest and dissatisfaction, the net result of which has been to increase the tariff reaction.

The sentiment of nationality which is in essence anti-foreign is most marked in those new states which have been created by the treaty of peace. The unfortunate consequence of the treaties of peace has been that a large number of new states have been created, without sufficient attention having been paid to the possible effect of an increase in the number of European frontiers on the economic prosperity of the Continent as a whole. The actual consequences of the creation of states all imbued with strong feelings of hostility towards other members of the European community has been in the particular case of the succession states of Austria-Hungary nothing short of disastrous, and one of the most urgent reforms in Central Europe is a lowering of the tariff walls and a sweeping away of the innumerable prohibitions on import and export which now hamper any rational solution of the Central European problem. In South America and the British dominions the desire to build up industries as a supplement to agriculture is an additional force.

A further difficulty in the way of free trade in the modern world lies in the absence of any one strong centre which is completely free trade in outlook. Holland and England were the two great free-trade areas, and although it cannot be said that protection has gained a complete victory in either of these areas, the forces making for free trade have been weakened in both. The incorporation into the British customs system of the principles of colonial preference, anti-dumping devices, and special protection to key industries has weakened the intellectual case for free trade. A precedent has been created which may form the basis for further measures of the same kind in the future. In Holland it must be recognized that the proximity to the great German industrial area constitutes a constant pretext for demands for special legislation against exchange dumping. These demands have so far not been successful, but the Dutch political situation is a curious one and the future here is very uncertain.

It is the spirit of nationalism again which is influencing, both for good and for evil, the policy of the Government of India. The trend in India is clearly towards self-government, and is so far to be distinctly welcomed. But it must not be forgotten that young India is inspired, not by Adam Smith and the traditional policy of the United Kingdom, but by the theories of List and the sudden rise to power of the Empire of Japan. The result is that the

forces making for protection in India are very strong, and
are indeed so strong that the traditional power of the
Lancashire cotton industry over the tariff policy of the
Government of India has gone, never to return. We
must expect, therefore, as a result of these political and
psychological factors that the Government of India will
move more and more towards protection, and in fact the
report of the recent Tariff Commission in India is only an
ample confirmation of this analysis.

It may perhaps be asserted that in the principles laid
down in the covenant of the League of Nations with
regard to the treatment of mandated territories a new
rallying point for the principles of free trade has been
found. Under the covenant equality of trading oppor-
tunity to all members of the League has been laid down
as a general principle. Unfortunately these provisions
have been somewhat curiously interpreted in practice,
e.g. they have not prevented the incorporation of certain
mandated areas in the British preferential system, nor
will it be noted, do they admit German or Austrian traders
to equality with the rest of the world.

The swing to free trade, if it ever comes again, will
come, it is to be feared, not as a result of a general grasp
of free-trade principle, but as a result of practical dissatisfaction with the workings of the tariff system in the
post-war world. Since that experience is disappointing
the advocates of free trade are not absolutely wanting.
The very increase in the total number of European frontiers
makes the working of protection more irritating and more
cumbersome, and the loss of trade and markets which
results from tariff barriers has already led to a notable
victory of free trade in the case of the West African
differential export duties, which have had to be abolished.
As the feeling of international tension which the war has
left behind it gradually dies down, as the fears induced by
disorganized currency systems are diminished by the
gradual restoration of sounder currencies, room will be
given for sounder views on the merits and benefits of
unrestricted international trade. The fear that England
will be flooded by cheap German " reparations " goods

and the similar fear that the United States will be flooded by cheap goods representing payment of the American debt, will probably be removed as the impossibility of making these enormous payments comes more and more clearly to be realized. The temptation to impose tariff barriers will disappear when it is realized that the expectations of indefinitely continued payments of large sums from debtors to creditors is a psychological, if not an economic, impossibility. Meanwhile, for the student of economics the lesson to be learned is that of patience. It is useless to argue with a fever-stricken patient. The general principles upon which the English school of free trade has based its case have not been affected by the events of the last few years, though free-traders must recognize that the circumstances of the world make the recognition of those principles very much more difficult. It has sometimes been a temptation for free-traders to base their case upon particular circumstances of time and place. The events of the last few years should convince them that such *ad rem* argumentation is out of place, and that the victory of their cause is likely to be more secure in the long run if it is based upon an appreciation of general principle and not on the inconveniences of a particular set of circumstances.

INDEX

Printed by Jarrold & Sons, Ltd., Norwich